G000270744

For *Jane Dorner*

Presented as confirmation of full attendance
and successful participation in the three-day
INTENSIVE BUSINESS SPEAKING AND PRESENTATION
COURSE, in London *January 24-26, 1990*

With sincere good wishes for many winning
presentations, from the Author-Director

FIoD, MBIM, MCIM, MIPR

How to Make Effective Business Presentations—and Win!
A practical A-to-Z guide

How to Make Effective Business Presentations— and Win!

A practical A-to-Z guide

John May

Director: John May School of Business Speaking and Communication

Illustrated by
Ray Jelliffe

McGRAW-HILL BOOK COMPANY

London · New York · St Louis · San Francisco · Auckland · Bogotá
Guatemala · Hamburg · Lisbon · Madrid · Mexico · Montreal
New Delhi · Panama · Paris · San Juan · São Paulo · Singapore
Sydney · Tokyo · Toronto

Published by
McGRAW-HILL Book Company (UK) Limited
MAIDENHEAD · BERKSHIRE · ENGLAND

British Library Cataloguing in Publication Data
May, John.
How to make effective business presentations—and win!
1. Communication in management
2. Communication in organizations
I. Title
658.4'5   HF5718
ISBN 0-07-084587-5

Library of Congress Cataloging in Publication Data
May, John.
How to make effective business presentations—and win!
1. Communication in management.
2. Public speaking.
3. Business report writing.
I. Title.
HF5718.M39   1983   658.4'52   82-20863
ISBN 0-07-084587-5

Copyright © 1983 John May. All rights reserved. No part of this publication may be reproduced, stored in a retrieval system, or transmitted, in any form or by any means, electronic, mechanical, photocopying, recording, or otherwise, without the prior permission of the original copyright holder and of McGraw-Hill Book Company (UK) Limited

2345 M.C. 887

Typeset by Phoenix Photosetting, Chatham
Printed and bound in Great Britain by
Mackays of Chatham Ltd

The very proper Latin motto of this book is

'AUDACTER DICTUM JAM VICTUM'

of which the reasonably accurate schoolboy translation is
'Boldly Spoken Wins a Jammy Victory'

CONTENTS

Preface

About how to use this book to improve your presentations

Short of speaking from the dock on a murder charge, I can't think of anything that comes heavier than giving an important business presentation. Speaking informally to even the kindliest group makes many business people nervous. Presentation is considerably more stressful than that.

First, the audience is well informed and often already has its own anxieties and prejudices concerning the facts and ideas being expressed. Second, the bosses are usually present in force, both from the presenting and the client sides. Third, it is the audience's hundreds, thousands, even millions of pounds or dollars that you as presenters are proposing to spend.

US companies put great weight on presentations. 'They are the most structured, directed and controlled form of human communication,' said David L. Woods, of the US Navy Department, Washington, when we discussed it. Probably the most harrowing presentations, therefore, are those staged by the European end of American companies. What these guys from the USA call '*pree–sentation*' makes strong men quake.

This book is designed to quell the quakes, set you free, and help you win. If he can take part in a business conversation, make a telephone call, or write a letter, almost any executive can learn to present well. But without guidance, the job can be a nightmare. Here the guidance is provided in a uniquely helpful style, in alphabetical order under more than a hundred headings. This format has real practical advantages. First, you can look up in half a minute any section which deals with a problem needing instant solution. Next, you are not committed to reading right through a book to find the part you want. And finally, the treatment, although authoritative, is not stodgily solemn. So you can enjoy dipping into sections (complete in themselves) when you have no time for a longer read.

I have tried to make the book entertaining and stimulating. But the basic purpose is serious: how to make effective business presentations—and win!

Ongar, Essex
John May

Acknowledgements

To every single one of hundreds of men and women delegates on scores of speaking and presentation courses—run in London for my own School of Business Speaking, at Maidenhead for the College of Marketing, in Brussels for Management Centre Europe, and in-company for dozens of top organizations in a rich variety of industries all over the UK and many elsewhere in Europe—I owe thanks for inspiring the distilled ideas and advice given in these pages.

To the hardworking and enthusiastic teams of young presenters I trained at the Regent Advertising Club of London, who won the Advertising Association's national speaking competitions five years running, I owe my transformation from Fleet Street journalist to international lecturer.

To my friend Eric Webster, I owe this new career when he offered me my first engagement as a professional lecturer at a top London advertising agency. And to my friend Ray Jelliffe, originally from the same agency, I owe grateful thanks for his felicitous humorous illustrations in this book.

Accents and dialects. Why it pays to regard yours as a virtue

One of the happiest memories of my first visit to the USA was to do with the accent. In their rich pronunciation of our mutual language, amused Americans repeatedly demanded: 'Say something in *English*, John!' Along with travelling 3000 miles to see them, my London pronunciation was a social passport.

Any presenter who regards his or her accent as a handicap (as many tell me they do) is wrong. Today, our radio, records, TV, films, telephones, and travel have made the world's variety in accents a pleasure everyone savours. Accents can be used in presentation to give different effects. Lancastrians sound kind, confident and optimistic. West of England accents are rich like cream. Yorkshiremen are blunt.

A presentation with several speakers who talk alike soon grows monotonous. A good American or other accent is a refreshing change from the local vocal sound.

Possibly there is still one way of speaking which can handicap you: too 'good' an accent. Edward Heath is one English political leader who had to tone it down.

If your first language is not English, then probably the way you pronounce words, and the particular lilt of your sentences, will have a piquant fascination. Great French artistes of the past were at pains to preserve their Gallic intonation for English audiences. But even here, there are shades of sound which can irritate, and should be avoided. The journalist, Olga Franklin, wrote wittily of a Fräulein who complained about the Herr Doktor: 'He keeps saying "zis and zat" instead of "dis and dat".'

Being your natural self pays best. When young Norman Birkett came from the north of England to Cambridge University, he gradually slipped into standard southern English. A great advocate, he became one of Her Majesty's judges, Britain's Lord Justice of Appeal. His verdict on accent: 'Nothing is worse than the artificial veneer some people adopt in order, they think, to give an impression of breeding and education. Exaggerated speech to create an effect is ridiculous.'

Employ your accent with pride. Change only those isolated words which others find ugly or hard to understand. Apart from such polite adaptation, cherish the rest as an essential part of that personality which others appreciate in you.

Acting. Has it a useful part in business presentations?

One had to be an inarticulate heavyweight talking to a youth club about boxing; another a famous pop singer addressing a choir school about plain-song. For an end-of-year fun exercise in a speaking group, we gave each aspirant an improbable impromptu speaking assignment. Instead of being flummoxed, even the shyest let themselves go nobly.

Merely to be themselves is, for some immature business speakers, to be indeterminate, vague, inconclusive, and innocuously dull. The truth is that their characters have not developed 'personality muscle'. They have little experience, mild opinions, ordinary ideas, and no strong feelings. But, as our fun session demonstrated, they can become useful presenters if taken out of themselves and given a clear role to play. They need a strongly creative person to script their presentation and produce them in the part. They can then play the role like an actor and will probably appear more effective than merely being themselves.

The best part for anyone to play is that of the role he is supposed to be fulfilling in the organization. A judge may privately have acute sympathy for the man in the dock, but though he may exercise some mercy, nevertheless he must see justice done. That is his job. Most people do merge into and fulfil their roles eventually.

When good presenters have the facility for writing a part and developing a personality, they can likewise strengthen their performance and persuasiveness by delineating their role more sharply. Sometimes, as we know, this *persona* even grows to be at variance with the private character of such an individual. Sometimes it takes over.

As George Du Maurier portrayed in his famous novel *Trilby*, where Svengali mesmerizes a girl to fame as a singer, women generally take to such acting roles more readily than men. Males are frequently less flexible. Unless they have been brainwashed in depth, however, such players should be submitted only with the greatest care to the embarrassment of discussing or answering questions about their presentations. Usually this is a function for the man pulling the strings, Mr Mastermind, who knows all the answers.

Action visuals speak louder than words—if they work

Action can dramatize the points of your presentation in unforgettable fashion. At a sales conference in Liverpool, a food

3

company stationed a man on stage at a small table with a pile of dinner plates. When speakers put over a main fact, he raised a plate in the air, cried 'That's another smashing point!' and crashed it with a seven-pound hammer.

The action is still remembered; the points are probably forgotten. But, at the time, it accomplished the object of arousing an audience of salesmen.

Breaking a pencil in two, tearing up a cheque or currency notes, crushing a cardboard box underfoot, and relevant violence or destruction impresses most audiences. The Who rock group originally became famous by smashing their guitars and amplifiers on stage—at enormous cost.

Fire always fascinates. A demonstrator from the Safety in Mines Research Establishment ignites in mid-air a series of ascending soap bubbles to show the explosive danger of methane gas.

Throwing appropriate and harmless objects excites and dramatizes. Coins tossed into an audience (which they scramble to pick up) contrasts with 'many times that amount being wasted hourly in our industry'.

A glassful of water flung across the stage makes everyone sit up. Sir Alan Herbert dramatically threw his divorce bill onto the floor of the House of Commons when it was talked out. Another time, an MP tossed down a carton: 'One mandate the Government *never* got was to sell the British Empire for a packet of cigarettes!' he cried.

Sir Bernard Miles, founder of the Mermaid Theatre, tells how in a scientific educational show for children, 'we hung four small parachute-harnessed boys from a steel joist like joints of meat, then hung one little girl four times further away from the fulcrum, thus proving that one female is equal to four males'. Sir Bernard's popular science tricks were double guarded against failure. But even simple acts can go wrong.

Giant objects rolled onto a dance floor, inflated carnival figures and animals, showgirls emerging from polystyrene pies—these smack of circus acts, are costly, and need careful handling because they can go badly wrong. A mayor pulled from his pocket the silk 'handkerchief' chosen to match his blue silk even-

4

ing suit: it was his wife's knickers. A boxer, leaping into the ring at the World Sporting Club, London, flung off his robe and raised his gloves in high salute to 5000 fans—but had forgotten to put his shorts on.

While the band played 'Hail to the Chief' and President Harry Truman strode to the lectern, a lady released a flock of 'doves of peace'. One almost sat on the chairman's head, while others hit walls and balcony and plunged to the floor. Only Truman's vitality as a speaker saved the day.

There is scope for considerable creative imagination in this kind of 'action' visual aid. The essentials are: something that is simple and inexpensive to arrange, that won't go wrong, and that makes your point dramatically and appropriately.

Advocacy. The problem when you are not convinced yourself

'If I believed in this proposition, gentlemen, I would commend you to buy it. But frankly, in my view, it is not good enough, and I advise you not to accept what my colleagues say. Save your money.' Few presenters when sober have ever dared come out with anything like this. But sometimes you may be tempted. What should you do?

This is a question that worries many young executives. Some people are totally unable to put forward a view they don't strongly hold. Others more flexible in mind can argue for or against a case with equal eloquence and ease.

Whatever your character, I would say that you should decide either to accept or reject the role you are asked to play well before presentation day. When it comes to the presentation, the honest way is to be loyal to the team. You must use all your talents to be as persuasive as possible. And you should never disagree with your fellow presenters publicly in the client's presence.

There is one saving fact to remember. Like a barrister in court, you are merely pleading a cause. Advocacy is your job. Do realize that you are *not* the judge or jury. Making the final judgement on the facts and suggestions you present is the client's job. He is the judge.

Alcohol for speakers. May's formula to assess the right dosage

When I first met my potato-farmer friend George Scales, he said: 'It takes me three months to prepare a speech—and two bottles of whisky to deliver it.' George was sent to me by his doctor to abate his nervousness. He had won a Nuffield award to tour potato farms in Europe and the USA learning and lecturing about the methods in both continents. But he was terrified of speaking.

Training in presentation lowered his alcohol index to normal. He began to enjoy speechifying. The Scales family joined in, and his wife, daughter, son, and manager all made winning speeches. George himself is now a regular speaker on agricultural subjects. Not long ago he did a brilliant half-hour solo television programme.

Alcohol in moderation is a legitimate way many presenters calm undue nervousness. It acts as a tranquillizer.

A group of Scots engineers at Brentwood, in Essex, asked how many drams a man should take before speaking. We decided that research would reveal how many made him happy. Then, with 'H' equalling happiness, the right number of drinks was 'H minus One'. One over the 'H' brings other problems besides speaking— such as standing up!

Some presenters find alcohol a useful post-rhetorical restorative. A good example comes from my friend Cedric Dickens (ex-

International Computers). Great grandson of the famous author, he records in his book *Drinking with Dickens* that 'When exhausted by his public readings of his novels, Charles Dickens used to have an egg beaten up in sherry'.

Applause. Using it to improve people's presentations

You are shaking with nerves and baggy-eyed with overnight rewriting. You rehearse your presentation to the full board of directors and the response is . . . silence. Arguments develop about your script, ignoring you as if you were a robot; or you are attacked viciously about nit-picking points without the right of reply.

A man or woman who has rehearsed a presentation should at least be sincerely and publicly thanked by the biggest boss present. If there are more than half a dozen listening, approval cannot easily be expressed verbally by all. But there is an easy and highly effective way: a round of applause.

Sports crowds, politics, show business—they all use the heartening effect of hand-clapping. But the world of business, complaining about low morale at all levels from factory floor to over-taxed boardroom, stays pinch-penny mean with approbation.

Ready applause is the immediate reward in speaking and presentation which helps condition the performer into feeling that it is worth while. It costs little, and depletes no resources. It brings a flush of pleasure and reinforces motivation. It works because it is *instant*. Dr Mary Willard, training animals at Harvard Psychology Department, proved that learning is helped most when the reinforcer (reward) follows in 0.4 seconds of correct performance. Humans react the same to the easy *quick* reward of hand-clapping. It grooves success into a habit.

7

Attention graph. How to keep interest up and stop it sagging

The managing director of a famous film production company told us how an epic is planned to grip the audience. The interest starts high, then is allowed to relax slightly before being stimulated to a new peak. The process of alternating provocation and release continues as the excitement grows ever higher, finally climaxing at the end.

If we could graph the attention given by the audience to a presentation, it should follow a similar path. My theory of applying showmanship ideas to presentations is that any form of communication that continues through time is likely to be successful if we can make it follow the attention graph of a good film.

Unfortunately, many presentations take the weary road followed by a school class during a normal 45-minute period. Interest begins high in the first 5 minutes. In the next 10 it drops only slightly. Then, at 15 minutes, it falls increasingly steeply and bottoms out at 30 to 35 minutes. A minor peak arises at 40 minutes in expectation of the bell for the next lesson.

A brilliant presenter can hold an audience's attention for an hour. How is it done? The vital parts of the message should be trailed at the beginning and brought out strongly at the end, the times when attention is highest. But, more important than all, we should look to the interest graph at the stage, two-thirds of the way through, when it sags lowest. This applies whether the duration be an hour, a day, or even a week.

Can we achieve a change of pace? Different, more exciting visuals? A bit of role-playing with a second speaker? Tear up and throw away your notes? Stage an interruption? Ring a handbell? Make an unexpected call (prearranged) for drinks for the audience?

Alas, at this dull point, some presentations bring on a man with a voice like a subdued blue-bottle fly, with illegible visuals. Interest dies.

What can be done in the reverse direction was dramatically demonstrated by a quiet speaker at a conference about army radio. He suddenly switched on a film of hand-to-hand battle with ear-shattering sound effects of explosions. People in the audience ducked, but interest shot sky high.

Audience accord and control. How to make people listen and like it

'It's entirely a technical business,' remarked Noël Coward, the great actor-playwright. 'You have got to control the audience, and they must never control you. They've got to do what you tell them.'

How do you achieve audience control and accord in presentation? Part of your success will arise from *research* and *planning*. The rest will come from how you manage your *monitoring* during the actual face-to-face delivery.

1. *Research.* Before a line of your script is prepared, you need to find out everything you possibly can about the audience. You can hardly ask too many preliminary questions. Compose a checklist of matters that seem vital to the occasion. How many will be present? Who else is speaking? What is the order of appearance? How long is allowed? What is the strong common interest and viewpoint of the audience? Are they male, female, or mixed? Mature—or young and aggressive?

'The average top director is 56 years old,' says a management survey. 'He has been a director for 9 years, and sits on a board with 11 colleagues . . . . About 70 per cent of such directors went to public schools, and 50 per cent to universities.'

A more ebullient good fellowship greeted me one evening in London at Greenwich Round Table (all men under 40) where I was invited by my advertising friend John Billett. Said their president: 'A pity our speaker–killer is not here tonight. We always have a go at you, you know. Last meeting, we had the speaker crying!' We enjoyed a hilarious and hard-hitting session. But I could have been at risk through not discovering in advance this audience's habit of high-spirited heckling.

2. *Planning.* When you have researched your audience's characteristics and needs, then you can tailor your presentation to cater for them. Like any selling job, it is a matter of putting forward what you want to say in terms of the *benefits* to them.

Everyone in an audience questions to himself, consciously or unconsciously, 'What's in this for me?' If the treatment reveals facts and ideas near to the audience's hearts, pockets, sympathies, wishes, fears, hungers, ambitions, needs, advantages . . . then they will listen. If not, the best you can expect is cool uninvolved good manners. A famous MP wrote that audiences tend to give the performer the benefit of the doubt: 'A dull speaker, like a plain woman, is credited with all the virtues, for we charitably suppose that a surface so unattractive must be compensated by interior blessings.'

The first commandment for presenters, however, is 'Thou shalt not be dull'.

3. *Monitoring.* Good delivery is the third secret of achieving audience accord.

First, the speaker must be clear in his mind what response he wants from his listeners and set about getting it. The situation is an action–reaction one. His action provides the input and the signals; their response should be the reaction he requires. If what he wants from them is possible; if he shows clearly what he wants; if he warms them to the emotional level at which they are ready to give it—then he will have their accord, and everyone will be happy. A good speaker plays an audience like a trained organist plays on his instrument. He is in control. Keep this idea of *audience control* clearly in your mind.

Second, the speaker can monitor how far he is succeeding by eye contact with the audience's faces. All those faces out there are 'dials' that you can read like the instrument panel of a car. There is no short cut to assessing an audience's response. The only way is to speak as frequently as possible, to as varied an assortment of groups as possible, and continually to study them. You need to become a psychologist. And in this instance a psychologist is someone who goes to a strip show and watches the customers.

Third, then, we have to study how to interpret these feedback signals of facial response, body attitude, etc. The laughing audience is totally receptive, at least for the moment. If they are smiling and nodding, sitting forward on their chairs, they are taking it in. If their eyes tend to glaze over, you probably need to improve the ventilation, especially after lunch. When they frown, mutter, shake their heads, comment to one another, these are disagreement signals. Say 'I see that not everyone agrees'. Promise 'In a moment we will find out why'. Never ignore negatives.

Finally, it is important to end before they tire. Even if a presentation is intended to be immortal, there is no need for it to go on for ever. Watch out for the watch-checker, the man who puts his spectacles away, the delegate who sneaks a look at his air ticket, and the official who shuffles his papers into a neat stack. In spirit they have finished—even if you have not.

Audience accord is that happy state of rapport when they respond to the slightest subtlety from you and when you too can take a delicate hint from them.

Audience arithmetic. What is wrong with Moses's 10 commandments?

Presenters persistently cram too much into their presentations. They are eager to give value and because of all that preparation, they want to show how hard they have worked. The result is boring, confusing, and exhausting. They need to learn the brutal truth about May's audience arithmetic concept.

After Moses split the Red Sea and got the Israelites out of

Egypt, he brought them (Exodus 20) the 10 commandments. It is a terrific code of laws, backed up with tough corollaries and penalties which many people have forgotten.

Generations have lived by the commandments. Yet few people I meet can remember and recite them. If they try to write them down, they end with 9 or 11. Why? Because most of us cannot readily recall 10 items from a mental list. Indeed, if we are told things by word of mouth, our audience arithmetic counts them off: *one . . . two . . . three . . . a lot . . . far too many*. After that, audience arithmetic (unless aided by visuals, mnemonics, or documents) gives up. This is a fact of presentation life which no speaker can afford to neglect. At best, five points is all that most of the audience will recall, and then only with difficulty after the first three. The New Testament condenses the commandments to two, an excellent example for presenters.

B

Bad temper can be vitally useful—if you don't make a clown of yourself

On a famous occasion, USSR Premier Nikita Kruschev pulled off a shoe in the UN and hammered the desk with it. 'We will bury you!' he roared in Russian.

A touch of table-thumping temper can add weight and flavour to your business presentation—if it is controlled. Strong feeling makes for exciting speaking. As my old friend, *How to Win Friends* Dale Carnegie, put it: 'Walk up behind the most inarticulate man in the world and kick his legs from under him, and he'll rise and make the speech of his life.'

Three precautions. First, it is wiser to attack principles rather than people.

Second, think before you bellow, and avoid taking up a last-ditch position from which there is no room to manoeuvre.

Third, your righteous indignation should be seen to be restrained. It is more powerful that way. Harold Macmillan, at the UN, deflated Kruschev's thumping threats by asking innocently 'May we have a translation of that?'

The best target for vociferation is an enemy, whether actual or imagined. Nothing brings people together better than to find they

13

are mutually threatened. Every presenter needs an enemy to inveigh against, preferably one who *can't* be killed off.

Blackboard (and whiteboard) chalk-n-talk presentation tricks

A sociological history of the blackboard could make an enlightening thesis. A hotel near St Albans, Hertfordshire, possesses an antique example made (at a guess) by a farmcart builder about 1840. The oaken easel legs are hobbled with a blacksmith's chain. The board is iron bound and weighs half a hundredweight. When I last used it, a joker had sawn half-through the pegs. The board crashed down on my toes. I fell through the easel with an agonized yell and the audience applauded wildly.

Blackboards in hotel meeting rooms are notoriously ill-maintained. Check the easel to ensure it won't do the splits. See that the pegs are not self-ejecting. Choose the less greasy side. Look out for stub ends of decapitated drawing pins in the surface which will rip your fingers. Clean with a warm wet sponge if available, and dry with a clean (not chalk-sodden) cloth. Ensure that you have chalks long enough to hold.

Very much a workshop tool, and certainly not for super-slick presentation, chalk-n-talk can nevertheless be elegant and convincing in the hands of a trained user.

The back-wall fixed board, often in dark green with an aluminium ledge, is a handy hold-all of information, but tends to become a background. An easel blackboard, more prominent but with a confined surface, acts as a stronger focus of attention. Whiteboards can be used in much the same way.

To improve your blackboard layout skill (which is where many users fail), plan out the visual on a sheet of 8 by 10 inches quarto paper. On the board itself, rule in horizontal pencil lines and vertical margins, with curves and diagrams, in advance. They will not be seen at a distance. Draw over the invisible pencil in chalk and impress the audience with your visual mastery.

If you are writing up points, keep to quick keywords, not sentences; if figures, don't omit the units—dollars, pounds, tonnes, miles. Avoid talking to the board, back to the audience, which is both ineffective and unmannerly.

There are two ways to point to what is on the board. One is using your left hand, and keeping back to avoid trespassing on audience sight-lines. The other is to press your breast-bone against the board's edge, and point with the forward hand. In either style, stand in front of the board, or wipe it off, when you want to maintain your personal initiative by switching off the visual.

Blackout and other memory failures. What to do when stumped

Blackout, the nightmare of suddenly suffering a complete mental blank, normally happens only once in a presenter's lifetime, and to some people never. But minor failures of memory and saying the unintended—these are relatively common. Millions watching TV heard both the Prince and Princess of Wales make slips during their marriage responses in St Pauls Cathedral, for instance.

The chairman of a Conservative constituency dinner was perhaps suffering from the strain of the occasion, when he and his members entertained the then Tory Prime Minister. The Premier spoke. Everyone applauded. The chairman summed up: 'You have heard our Prime Minister's inspiring words. And now it behoves us all to go out into the highways and byways, and work for the success of the *Socialist* Party!' Appalled astonishment! Had the ground opened before the chairman, at that moment, he would surely have dived in. I know his name and constituency, but for mercy's sake won't give them.

The mental machine just slips a cog or two. Pressure, fluster, fatigue, drink, or psychological hang-ups are all possible causes. What can you do?

First, never leave vital facts, figures, names, or titles to the vagaries of memory under pressure. Hold onto a note of them, lettered large. Said David Dimbleby, famous BBC TV personality: 'Write down even the name of the president, in case you forget it when interviewing him.'

Second, whatever happens, never show embarrassment in front of an audience. It makes them terribly uncomfortable, because they don't know how to react. In the middle of a sermon, our village parson once stopped and said: 'I'm terribly sorry. I've forgotten what I was saying.' He turned cheerfully to his wife, who was at the organ, and asked: 'What was I talking about, darling?' She told him, and he went on. Nobody was the slightest bit upset. All the congregation, in fact, was smiling.

Body language in clients. Do-it-yourself guide to messages it conveys

The evening grew late, but 12 participants at the presentation leaned forward, sat on the edge of their chairs, and listened eagerly. 'They didn't need to say anything,' commented the chief presenter. 'We knew from their behaviour we'd got 'em.'

All oral communicators read the body language of audiences, some without realizing, others with keen awareness. It pays you as a presenter to study what your clients say with this form of dumb eloquence. Before any comment is uttered, you can be forewarned that someone is less than motivated, or that another mildly disagrees. Better still, you can tell when you've hit a good line.

The client who critically examines the ash on his cigar, or gazes at a high cloud passing outside the window, is certainly wandering in spirit. Another, fingering a protruded lip, clearly signals doubt. The executive who sits up suddenly has had his interest pricked, almost as if with a pin. Jungle gorillas show threat by frowning. Boardroom guerillas ditto. But this is not a dictionary of body language, which is by no means new. 'There's language in her eye, her cheek, her lip,' Shakespeare makes the Greek commander Ulysses say in *Troilus and Cressida*. 'Nay, her foot speaks. . . .'

The body language vocabulary varies in different cultures and from one person to another. As scientific observers point out, nods and headshakes that mean 'Yes' and 'No' in Britain are reversed to 'No' and 'Yes' further east.

Study your client to interpret what his particular song-without-words is saying.

Does a top man cross his legs and waggle the suspended toe when impatient? Get your presentation moving faster into more interesting areas.

'Beware when he begins to twinkle benignly,' a junior was instructed about a certain chairman. 'He thinks he's roped you with a logical lasso.'

The man sitting elbow on table, hand over mouth, is reserving his judgement. He is a cautious buyer or may be a merchant banker. The nodder, with eyebrows raised welcomingly, is a supporter who likes your proposition.

Body language is only occasionally a total replacement for words. It provides supplementary clues to understanding. Certainly the girl who rubs her eyes may be shy, but don't overlook that it may be mild conjunctivitis.

You won't normally need to choreograph your client's facial or bodily expressions. Don't let such signs frighten you. React to them positively. Read them to improve your understanding of him.

C

Cardboard chart is the old faithful of visuals

For a stalwart long-life visual, which can hardly go wrong in any circumstance, it is hard to beat the cardboard chart. Different from the upright style flipchart, it is usually arranged horizontally (landscape, not portrait), like the blackboard. What was once 30 inches wide by 20 inches high is now, of course A1 size, in centimetres, or about 32 by 23 inches.

Charts can be enlarged photographically from typewriting or typesetting. Lettered by an artist, especially in colour, they are magnificent but sometimes expensive. The beauty of them is that they are no trouble to show. Modern boards are lighter than the old style. You can prop them anywhere—on a shelf, a desk, a table, an armchair—any place where the light shines on them.

They are easy to see; can be scribbled on; can be brought nearer; can be photographed up or down. Kept simple, and not over-crowded with data, nothing can beat them for clarity and multi-usage.

CCTV. How to use it to build confidence for presenters

If Robert Burns, the great Scottish ploughman poet, were brought back today from 200 years ago, you could show him his wish come true:

> O wad some Pow'r the giftie gie us
> To see oursels as others see us!
> It wad frae mony a blunder free us,
> And foolish notion.

When you tell rehearsing novice presenters that they perform well, they like to hear it, but seldom truly believe you. They know how desperate they feel, and cannot believe that their chaotic thoughts are not clearly betrayed on their faces.

Electronics has answered Robbie Burns' prayer (made incongruously, it is sometimes forgotten, in a poem about a louse crawling on a lady's hat). Rehearsing presenters can see themselves as others see them—by action replay on closed-circuit television (CCTV).

There are bad ways and better ways to do this. The boring method is to stand the presenter in front of a fixed focus camera, with no cameraman, and tell him to make his presentation direct. When you play it back on the monitoring screen from the videotape, the result is a dull 'talking head' presentation—generally very wooden.

No presenter normally focuses all his attention on one fixed audience-eye which can give him nothing in return but an optical glare. So his performance in such circumstances is likely to be noticeably static, or at the other extreme to appear artificially and hysterically animated. It is unlikely to appear natural.

A better way is for the cameraman and camera to be part of a group, maintaining the role of unnoticed onlooker. The presenter discusses points with this and that person in the audience-group, doing most of the talking himself but a little listening, too. He

'O wad some Pow'r the giftie gie us To see oursels as others see us.'
Robbie Burns' wish comes true in presentation training.

speedily becomes unaware of the camera, and reacts naturally to the group. The cameraman meantime goes into close-up when the presenter's face is eloquent; pulls out to a wider view when he is gesturing or using a visual; zooms in briefly to isolate any peculiar mannerism—ear-pulling or table-tapping.

When this is played back from the videotape, the monitor provides a good show. Also the whole rehearsing group is involved and so will be ready to watch, appreciate, and analyse.

It must be emphasized that this is not making a presentation into a TV performance, but is using CCTV as a peephole to see a presenter in action. It gives the performer a whole new exciting self-awareness.

Checklist for progressing presentations through to the end

A hare and a mare, countryfolk say, makes a year: one month of gestation for leverets; eleven for a foal. The gestation period of your presentation may vary from a mouse's to a mammoth's. But, much or little, six phases must happen, or you'll get an abortion.
1. Conception and setting objectives.
2. Drafting and roughing out visuals.
3. Briefing and rehearsing presenters and back-up.
4. Briefing the audience.
5. Giving presentation.
6. Follow-up activities.
Simple presentations are often pushed through in a devil-take-hindmost rush. The tool to ensure the progress of more complicated presentations through these stages *on time* is some version of the Gantt Chart. Henry L. Gantt invented this device for getting battleships built on schedule in the USA during the 1914 war. Critical path analysis (from Dupont) and PERT (the US Navy's

Program Evaluation and Review Technique) are refinements developed in the fifties.

The natural way to plan any large task is to start from the beginning and go step by step to the end. Gantt's better technique was to start with the completed end product and delivery date, then work back to fix developmental stages and starting dates.

Obviously, in preparing a presentation, you can have various jobs done at the same time. They are not an end-to-end series of tasks, but parallels. Some participants can be writing, for example, while assistants arrange dates and venues for rehearsals and performance.

There will be one job of irreducible length (possibly involving the conception and making of visuals) which dictates how long the whole preparation takes. This is the critical path, around and into the duration of which all other activities must fit. Working backwards from the presentation date, this is the job which dictates how soon we must start if we are to be ready on time.

A classic domestic example of a critical path is the cooking of the joint for Sunday lunch. In an orderly household, the time this takes is a period around and into which all other morning activities are fitted; otherwise lunch can become an accident that occurs any time up to 5.00 pm. Even then, providing such obvious needs as mustard or mint sauce can become last-minute jobs, because overlooked.

Checklists prevent omissions in presentation preparation. Each phase needs at least one set of check questions. Here are some basic ones, to which you can add your own.

1. *Conception and objectives.* What do we want *who* to do *when,* as a result of the presentation? What must we say and show to achieve this? How do we hope to measure our success?

Audience. What do we know or need to find out about them? Age? Economic status? Level of knowledge, intelligence, and sophistication? Emotional attitude? How many should be present? What decision can be expected of them?

Timing. How much advance notice of date does the audience need? What date, time of day, duration?

Venue and facilities. Room and seating? Telephone interruptions? Microphones? Foils, slides, film projector? Charts, chalkboards? Other aids? Documentation? Costs? Parking, reception, refreshment, toilets?

2. *Drafting words, planning visuals.* What facts and ideas have we to describe and show? Best way to do it? How much does audience know? Can we keep it simple? Authority for assertions and promises? Tough or tentative projection?

Reaction. What is sought? How to get questions? How will audience express opinion?

Outline of message. Who drafts wording and assembles visual ideas? With whom should outline be pre-checked?

How soon can complete presentation be written? How soon can finished visuals be commissioned?

3. *Briefing and rehearsing.* Who is preparing and handling the master-programme? What goes on it? Are operators briefed about visuals and other aids, lighting, etc?

Chairman. Does he fully understand running order? Introductions prepared? Link passages? Know timing? Know duties of other performers?

Performers and others. Are speakers and their parts prepared? What about other functions: reception, refreshment, microphone-handling?

Rehearsal. Early date to avoid panics? Time each part accurately by stopwatch? Encourage and make criticism and revision acceptable, not traumatic? Keep team working together to establish supportive comradeship?

4. *Briefing the audience.* What information is audience to receive in advance about the presentation and its purpose? Date, time, duration, venue, refreshment? Tell them what response is wanted? What follow-up with audience is planned after presentation?

5. *Giving presentation.* Start on time, keep time, finish promptly? Adequate breaks provided for?

Certain people assigned to the hospitable job of Mr or Miss Fix-it for audience?

Fail-safe arrangements if apparatus, presenters, audience, or other factors go awry?

Has overall chairman the recognized authority to interrupt, shorten, or edit the presentation while in progress?

6. *Follow-up activities.* Is someone briefed to thank (perhaps in writing) all those taking part?

What sound recording or minutes are to be kept of the presentation? In what form, if any, is it to be distributed to audience?

Hold an inquest, or ask for notes from participants, to plan follow-up action, analyse response, decide changes, or fix future presentations?

Every meal has a menu, whether or not it is planned or written down in advance. Every presentation has a progress plan, whether it be unwritten chaotic thoughts in the minds of a few frantic people, or a timed progress chart, which raises the right questions at the right time.

Adapt the above check stages and questions to your own level of need. Don't make your chart too detailed and fussy, or it will only hold up, not advance, progress. Use it as a think-pad for checking.

Given the right questions, all you need is sound judgement for finding answers and the ability to act on them. That's all!

Confidence. How you can build it for better presentation

You can learn a good deal about presentation by reading about it. But you can't overcome stagefright. To smile when your cheeks are stiff with fear, to bring the mist of faces into focus, to speak when your mouth feels full of glue—this you can only learn on your hind legs. You need a situation where you'll break no bones if you fall down. That way, it will be fun and you'll develop faster.

Bright young men and women in advertising, introducing themselves at the first evening in September at our speaking club, were told to say how they felt, and tell a little about themselves. 'Here I stand, a total wreck,' stammered one.

With quivery voice, another confessed: 'My heart is beating so hard, if I don't speak I'll explode.'

One couldn't give his name; he'd forgotten it. A companion slurred out: 'I'm undoubtedly the most fluid, if not the most fluent person present. My friends tell me I'm an eight-pint speaker. I'm here to reduce my handicap to two!'

By December, three months later, after meeting and speaking light-heartedly every Thursday evening, these youngsters were all competent, and a few were brilliant. Today many of them are directors of important British companies. Several have set up prosperous businesses in the UK and the USA. Every one of these successful men and women readily admits that presentation and speaking skills, learned when they were younger, have been invaluable to them in business and socially. The key to it all was regular speaking, even if only for two to three minutes a week, in a non-risk and enjoyable atmosphere.

Nobody need lack an opportunity to speak to an audience. Local authorities run evening classes. The cities have publicity and speakers' clubs. Young Farmers Clubs and others run contests. If you are lucky, your company may send you on a presentation course.

For practice without instruction, debating societies, discussion groups, parent-teachers associations, ratepayers, consumer groups, Round Table, Rotary, Women's Institutes, Townswomen's Guilds, and many more offer you opportunities to stand up and address a small gathering.

Seek out some regular practice, and you will soon get a kick out of it. The power of controlling an audience, of making them laugh or look serious according to your wishes, becomes intoxicating. As a British Medical Association publication put it: 'The speaker who begins to do this successfully is in complete charge of his surroundings . . . the master, the absolute boss.'

'This is strong medicine for the personality. Regular doses give an unforgettable taste of being no longer a mouse, but a mature adult.'

Courses on presentation—how and why they can help you

The virile strength of Ancient Greek education came from its being rooted in debate, question, and dispute. The flaccid weakness of much modern education is that it teaches pupils to absorb and regurgitate silently.

A young Doctor of Philosophy, with all the paper qualifications, was so shy that he was struck dumb at a presentation. And Lord Snowdon, a peer entitled to address the House of Lords, told a journalist: 'I can't make a worked-out speech.'

A good presentation training course breaks this sound barrier in three days.

1. Everyone makes numerous presentations, speeches, and contributions. Nobody is inhibited by business hanging on their performance. All are in it together and the atmosphere is enjoyable and enthusiastic.

2. Full play is given to the Chinese precept: 'What I see, I remember; what I do, I know.' Seeing and analysing other presenters' performances, and doing presentations themselves, fix the techniques provided by instruction.

3. By building on success and providing generous approbation in an optimistic atmosphere, participants are given a happy association to presenting, which they carry away with them.

The right speaking and presentation course can be a turning point in a man or woman's business career.

D

Delivery. Benefits and snags of the three main methods

How can you be as spontaneous and free when delivering a prepared presentation as when you speak impromptu? The answer is that many people find it difficult. Responsibility puts heavy boots on eloquence.

But you can *try* for freedom, and you will improve with practice. There are three main methods of delivering what has been prepared in advance:

1. From memory, as if spontaneously.
2. By reading from a complete script.
3. By taking a middle way between these two extremes.

Method One, speaking a memorized presentation, means giving a recitation. You are doing an act and the chances are that you are a reasonable speaker, but not so good as an actor. Apart from mouthing a mummified message, which may sound prefabricated, you may forget parts, or even omit them without realizing it.

After Winston Churchill once sat down wordless with a red face, he resolved never again to make a memorized speech without also having a full note available. 'If the memory fails,' he said, 'it is often impossible to start up the ordinary process of spontaneous composition.'

29

Method Two, reading a complete script, presupposes you can write speakable English. Given a speakable script, you need to be well practiced at bringing the words to life.

The two big snags in script-reading are:

1. Fading after the first well-rehearsed page.

2. Losing audience and confidence and gabbling off at high speed.

One new President of the USA read speeches so badly that he always seemed, they said, to be 'rushing for the final full stop'.

Reading is sometimes essential for a careful policy statement, or for broadcasting or recording where timing must be accurate to seconds. If you must read aloud, put some punch into it, maintain volume, and keep the pitch of the voice optimistic at the end of sentences.

The Middle Way (Method Three) is to speak from keywords and phrases. Keyword notes act like signposts for a motorist, as against reading a detailed map. The speaker can glance at them occasionally to see he is right. He does not need to read everything line by line, with eyes dangerously away from the audience.

An experienced presenter sometimes makes keyword notes on a complete script. With a pen of brightly contrasting colour, he underlines, rings, stars, numbers, and otherwise marks headings, sections and vital passages. With rehearsal, he can deliver spontaneously from this kaleidoscopic colour chart.

Given the right notes, you may not even need to use them. My old friend Arthur Secord, Professor of Speech at Brooklyn College, New York, was immensely popular with business audiences all over the USA. 'I never speak without notes. Only words or short phrases, and they are on cards 4 by 6 inches, held lengthways,' he told me. 'Many times I never refer to them in a 50-minute talk. But they are there . . . . They are like a crutch which is not needed, so long as it is within reach.'

Secord spoke as if responding to the plea of the fellow American who said 'Let us hear the ancient brimstone, the spoken words that burn and sear'. Great stuff!

But brilliance is not always best. Weight and persuasiveness are often more important in business. Among politicians Prime Minister Stanley Baldwin came across always as a man the people could trust. His stolid style prompted the economist John Maynard Keynes to remark to Kingsley Martin that they would never be premiers: 'Because neither of us has the capacity to write out a speech of impossible dullness, full of clichés and obvious truths, then learn it by heart and repeat it so slowly that everybody believes every word of it.'

Don't be too obviously eloquent in your presentation delivery. You may defeat your persuasive purpose. 'Take eloquence,' said the French poet Paul Verlaine, 'and wring its neck'.

Demonstration. Always try to show it rather than define it

This true story conveys a strong lesson for presenters. Because imports failed at source, the meat ration in Britain was even lower after the Hitler War than during the fighting. Said the Prime Minister: 'I want to see what the rations really are. I can't follow all those figures.'

So the Cabinet was shown a model of the meat, placed on a plate. Prime Minister: 'Well, that's quite a decent meal.'

Minister of Food: 'I'm afraid it's not a meal, Prime Minister.'

Prime Minister: 'What is it then—a day?'

Minister of Food: 'No, sir. A week!'

The food drive started. Demonstration always beats description and figures come to life when focused on a portion-for-one.

With a totally new concept, presentation without demonstration is a dead duck. Long before Sir Christopher Cockerell's Hovercraft became the famous sea-going craft of today, he showed me his newly discovered hover principle in his Norfolk Broads boat-yard. He depressed a small weighing scale with an air jet. It pushed down more heavily when passed through two concentric rings that made an air-enclosed cushion.

To Cockerell's far-seeing scientific mind, the implications were obvious. But others found them hard to see until the boat-builder, Desmond Truman, made Chris a working model. They took it to Whitehall and it chased a Civil Servant around a basement. Only then did the National Research Development Corporation begin to show financial interest. The demonstration had sold it.

No matter what it is you're talking about, if you can show it, or do it, or demonstrate it as a model or even diagrammatically, your presentation will have more impact.

Dirty stories seem to work well, but often backfire later

There is no denying the fact that dirty stories are popular currency with most people throughout the world. But for presentation purposes, if not totally banned, they should be employed with the utmost caution. A blue reference may seem to achieve instantaneous success. But afterwards people blame the teller for their own lapse from good taste in laughing.

If, despite this warning, you decide to bring in something salty, take a tip on how to use it. Says the professional expert, Britain's fabulous female impersonator, Danny La Rue: 'The essence of success with blue material is timing. If you sit on it, it becomes vulgar.'

Never forget that the occasion of Queen Victoria's most quoted remark, 'We are not amused,' was when an equerry told a questionable story at Windsor. The equerry and the story died. The Queen's reaction is long remembered.

Disadvantages of the spoken word. How presentations can overcome them

When you read this book, you can turn in a moment to any page you prefer. You can skim or absorb that page at any speed and in any order you like, even from the bottom upwards.

Listening to a presentation, you receive its message in the order decided by the speaker. You have no opportunity to skip forward, nor to turn back. He decides the speed, you must pay attention to what he says *now*, or miss it.

Presenters tend to concentrate on their own difficulties—confidence, coherence, marshalling of material. But the audience has problems, too, and the good presenter seeks to solve them.

The spoken word cannot be so complete, nor so condensed, as what is written. It should observe the constraints of audience arithmetic and speech structure. But it does have the extra advantages of vocal emphasis, facial expression, and gesture.

Visuals help the listener, but he must still remember their content when passed—he can't turn back to them. Similarly, calculations are for him mainly mental, so they must be easy to follow, and simple to accept.

What can best be perceived by listening are the simple trunk and branches of thought, with the foliage and twiggery of ifs and buts, qualifications, and exceptions stripped off. To achieve this takes a deal of hard work and clear thinking. If you have the message lucid and simple in your own mind, it is in a fit state to be passed in spoken words to others. If it is a forest of tangled concepts, they won't see the wood for the trees.

The spoken word has the ultimate great advantage of a personal presence. This commands respect from an audience in a way no printed word, no film, nor television reproduction can ever do. And that is why we make presentations instead of merely sending printed reports, pictures, and tapes. Furthermore, the living human being is someone we can talk back to and this *sharing* of thought is the true root of communication.

Dog words. Or to 'err' is human, but to pause divine

What are 'dog words'? This is my expression for those nonsensical reiterations and word-spacing noises that dog many presenters. 'Kind of', 'sort of', 'actually', 'err'—they jump up when not wanted. They trail aimlessly along with you, sniffing and fouling every signpost and milestone of thought. Often the victim doesn't realize he is dogged. He says, for instance, 'and so on and so forth'. He repeats it so often that people who first are irritated soon begin to grin, which means he has lost them.

Dog words annoy critical clients. They pollute presentation. In a recent one-day census I listed over 40 varieties which I won't call up in case they start following you.

If you are strong-willed and self-aware, you can monitor your own speaking and eliminate this rubbish. If you need help, it is easily provided by a friend who repeatedly checks you as a good trainer does a pulling dog. A silent pause is always a better spacer. It gives everyone time to think.

Doodlers are nature's way of telling you they won't play

Lord Hill tells a story in his autobiography about a Socialist who, angry about something, stormed into Prime Minister Attlee's room, holding forth passionately and at length. At the end, Clement Attlee looked up from his customary doodle, removed his pipe, and said: 'Can't agree with that.' End of discussion.

Beware of the doodler in your presentation audience, especially if he be high level. His enigmatic activity is not to be safely ignored.

Doodles, like dreams, games, graffiti, and even art are, from the psychologist's point of view, activities destined to relieve tensions. Doodling is the introverted adolescent form of self-indulgent art. The ex-headmaster of one of the largest grammar schools in Essex told me: 'Desktops in infants schools are free from doodles. But as pupils grow up, doodling proliferates in quantity and complexity until about age eighteen.

'The multi-doodled desks in grammar schools witness how the regime creates tensions without providing easy, natural outlets. Games are socially acceptable, but doodles tend to be secret, solitary and somehow shameful.'

What are their significance in presentations?

1. The doodler is waiting as patiently as he can, disguising his drive behind what is accepted as an idle, harmless, meaningless, but perhaps eccentric pursuit. The *Oxford Dictionary* compares the word 'doodle' with the Low German 'dudelkopf', a foolish person. Usually the doodler secretly wants to break away from, or break in on, what is being said.

2. Doodling in business is a mildly blameless displacement activity (providing it is on paper and not, for instance, scoring the polished boardroom table). It is the time bomb's inaudible tick. The strength of emotional pressure it disguises can be judged by the heavy patterning.

3. The doodler has gone partly non-verbal and turned some of his mind to abstract representation. He is displaying the withdrawal from verbal communication characteristic of some artists. When and if he does come to speak, therefore, he is likely to be vague or (with Attlee) laconic and blunt.

4. Sometimes the doodle is an exit into conscious fantasy, in which the doodler dreams—directly or indirectly—of, say, sailing or sex, food or drink, his garden, his bed, or other joys. When tackled, he will disturbingly have no comment to make or prefer to reserve his judgement.

You will glean little from rescuing a crumpled doodle to decipher it. Detailed significance resides only in the mind of the doodler, if indeed even he can bring it to conscious verbalization.

Dress and appearance can let you down. Make a cold-eyed check

That rampaging newsmaker of 200 years ago, John Wilkes, was a short, ribald, exceedingly ugly man with a startling squint. But he was socially successful. 'It takes me just five minutes,' he said, 'to talk away my face.'

While many business people are well-groomed, unfortunately some are sloppier than they realize—though clients inevitably notice.

A university professor with a string of degrees was shocked when he nearly lost a remunerative holiday lecture engagement on a cruise ship. 'You must agree,' the organizer said to me, 'he looks as if he sleeps in that suit.' The more senior the more embarrassing to tell a person to get his fingernails or hair cut. But if his scruffiness lets colleagues or company down, it must be done.

How clothes are worn conveys a message. Hands forever in trouser pockets gives a casual air, construed sometimes by seniors as lacking respect. Don't dive for your pockets so habitually that you can't speak otherwise. Slipping belts, unbrushed or deteriorating footwear, cigarette ash, tobacco, and food stains convey a tramp-like image. You need to be an evident genius to get away with it.

Undress is occasionally appropriate: jacket off for a workshop session—even displaying bright red braces, like the famous David Ogilvy. 'Strip aside pretentiousness and propriety,' said one of his creative directors, Stanhope Shelton. 'Get some panache into behaviour and appearance.'

Most presenters have a mental self-portrait which they should check for reality, preferably in a full-length mirror. In his book, *To the Point*, Woodrow Wyatt writes: 'I see myself as slim, good looking, with a strong, intelligent, handsome and kindly face. Why couldn't God see me like that?' Wyatt gives a realistic tip: he wears a bow-tie because falling food misses it 'and tends to land on the washable shirt.'

E

Ejaculation, premature. Novice presenters need restraint and timing

Too many terrified young presenters rush their audiences: they don't wait till people are settled and ready; they fail to allow listeners to tune into their voices; they neglect to arouse interest in their subjects; they just roar into the scene like a runaway motorbike smashing into a market stall. They suffer from verbal premature ejaculation.

There is a place for briskness. But these beginners speak so fast, and with such neglect of what the audience is feeling, that people *watch* them instead of listening.

In his memoirs, Lord Butler of Saffron Walden (then RA Butler) recalled intervening on a finance bill in the House of Commons. A senior member of the Government commented: 'That was a good speech, Rab. But you went too fast. You need not think everybody has a quick brain.'

Experienced professionals know how to pause to get attention before they begin. Mark Twain, the American humorous author of *Huckleberry Finn,* began at the age of 35 to make good money in his new profession of lecturing. In front of a full house at Utica, USA, he discovered the power of making the audience wait. He walked on stage and just stood patient and silent, saying nothing.

Then he realized he had hypnotized them just by his presence. There was sudden laughter and applause. 'I had captured them,' he said, 'for the rest of the evening.'

A bizarre tip on restraint and timing appears in *Brewer's Dictionary of Phrase and Fable*. The expression 'By the peacock!' was once an oath. It was regarded as blasphemous because the alleged incorruptibility of the peacock's flesh made it an allusion to the risen Saviour.

King George III, known as Farmer George, who was sometimes mad, had eccentric tricks of repetition. He ended every sentence with 'What? What?' When his ministers persuaded him to rehearse the King's speech to Parliament, he marked the fullstops with the then swear-word 'Peacock!'

The minister coaching him tactfully agreed that it was suitable for ending sentences. But he suggested that a King should not let his subjects hear it, but should whisper. 'The resulting pause at the close of each sentence,' records *Brewer's*, 'had an excellent effect.'

'Peacock' is now neither copyright nor blasphemous. It's available for any presenter who needs a 0.6-second pause to improve his timing. Pauses and restraint add punch to what you say.

Examples and case histories—using the parable technique

Attackers mugged a man on the Jericho road. They left him robbed, naked, and half dead. Even a priest passed without stopping. Then a Samaritan took the victim to an inn, tended him overnight, and paid the bill. 'Take care of him', he said in the morning, 'and whatsoever thou spendest more, when I come again, I will repay thee.'

Although you recognize the parable from St Luke, the point

here is about presentation, not religion. What happend was that a New Testament lawyer had asked a question demanding a definition of neighbourliness—*an abstract quality*: 'Who is my neighbour?' The answer he got was this vivid case history about being a good neighbour—so powerful that now, 2000 years later, there is a body of do-good people known to us as the Samaritans.

The communication moral for presenters is that the parable technique, as I call it, is the secret of making sense about any abstract quality, of which so many are talked about in business. Speaking generally about advertising, motivation, productivity, marketing, progress, planning, ambition, integrity, etc., is difficult. The example, anecdote, story, fable, instance, yarn, tale, or best of all the case history (a parable in modern business dress) makes it easy by coming down to concrete facts. Now we are on solid ground: a roadside with somebody hurt, but nobody stops. Gripping!

The beauty of the parable treatment is that a case history is easy to tell, easy to take in and understand, easy to remember. Search out and collect good case histories. They are a communication treasure.

Eye contact. If you abdicate it, you can lose the contract

At Gordonstoun School, in Scotland, which both Prince Philip and Prince Charles attended, a maths teacher was famous for writing up and working out a problem on the blackboard, explaining it verbally but never looking back at his pupils. One summer day, as he droned on, the small class including Philip slipped out of the open groundfloor window at the back and went rowing on the lake. They nipped in again seconds before the teacher finished, and he never knew.

Shy presenters who dislike and avoid looking at audiences can lose them almost as surely as the Gordonstoun man. Audiences are like sheep. When the shepherd does not keep his eye on them, they stray. The famous zoologist, Desmond Morris, in his fascinating field guide to human behaviour, *Manwatching,* describes cut-offs of eye contact that occur in presentation as well as socially. He defines them as Evasive Eye (wanders off), Shifty Eye (glances away), Stuttering Eye (flickering eyelids), and Stammering Eye (longer blinks). Dodging like this irritates an audience.

Appearing totally hypnotized by visuals or notes suggests that the speaker is unsure; looking at the floor, that he is ashamed; the ceiling, a prayer for inspiration; or out of the window, a desire to escape.

An audience rightly feels that a speaker who fails to look at them is emotionally rejecting their presence. After a time, they begin to gaze about, fidget, cough, doodle, read newspapers, or count things (patterns on the wall, bald heads, the speaker's mannerisms). Soon they mutter asides, start whispered conversations, smother laughter at little jokes, scrape their chairs, or even clap or laugh ironically.

Frequent soft-option advice is wrongly given to nervous novice speakers about where to look. Above their heads, or towards a friendly face. . . . There is *no* substitute for proper eye contact with the whole audience. Comedian Sir Harry Secombe, who is short-sighted, claims to be terrified of audiences. 'Fortunately, when I take my glasses off, they look like sago pudding, and I'm not frightened of sago pudding!'

Nobody should be ignored. Even those close beside you, under your elbows as it were, should be glanced at occasionally; so should any chairman or person in an isolated position. But your boss, or their boss, should *not* have the whole thing beamed solely at him. Let your gaze sweep back and forth across the whole audience like a beam of light, so that at frequent intervals you appear to be looking in turn briefly but directly at all present. *Miss nobody.*

Good eye contact with your audience keeps their attention rivetted on you. Scan their faces. Don't let them escape.

F

Fail-safe arrangements and attitudes that win when things go wrong

On the wall was a graph showing recent trends in packet-tea sales. Suddenly it fell off. 'You can *see* what's happened to the tea market,' quipped the marketing man who was presenting. Everyone laughed. From then on they were all totally with him.

In case things go wrong in a presentation, always be prepared with a fail-safe arrangement, and always seek profit from adversity.

If the high-stacked cans of soup avalanche down on you, crawl from under them and cry: 'As my next landslide shows . . . !' They'll love you for it.

An airline PR man was about to introduce an audio-visual tape-and-slide presentation to 200 travel agents. 'Terribly sorry, sir,' said his assistant in a scared whisper. 'The gear's not working.'

Through several previous showings, he had always carried a script in case this happened. Now he said: 'I'm grateful our robot presenter has gone on the blink, gentlemen, because it gives me the chance to talk to you today *personally*. . . .'

Accidents are often the presenter's friends. They make the audience feel pleasantly superior. Even the competition ice-skater who falls over can still score high marks. The boxer who takes a short count can still win the fight.

Fancy costumes and fitting garb makes vivid showmanship

Dressing up in fancy ways makes vivid communication. One presenter showing skirts brought in four matching office girls with nice legs. Although not mannequins, they weren't shy because each wore (as well as skirt and sweater) an artistic paper mask, held daintily on a wooden handle.

Any unusual costume piques interest: a Chelsea Pensioner in his red coat; a Scottish piper wearing the kilt; a model whose charms are clothed only in glued-on currency notes. A uniform, perhaps in period, always gains attention. A toreador, a cowboy, a cricketer in safety helmet. One sales manager wore his genuine fox-hunting pink, with breeches, boots, and spurs. Another joined the conference presentation disguised as a Chicago gangster.

Don't take it too far. A gang of stocking-masked 'bandits' who raided a presentation firing blanks from revolvers were not thought to be either dramatic or funny. Moral: know in advance how you'll look making your entrance—*and* how you will exit triumphantly instead of wrecking the show.

Figures and statistics. Presenting them to greatest advantage

Big business means big numbers. 'I like big figures,' confessed the benign old millionaire, Lord Thomson of Fleet, 'The more noughts the better.' Figures and statistics are therefore a vital part of presentation. But using them is hazardous. First there are the difficulties of audience, then those of representing figures visually, and finally that of giving them credibility.

For almost any audience, multiple figures (in more than one simple group) are difficult, if not impossible, to grasp and retain purely from hearing them said. We don't normally voice large numbers; we read them silently. A good presenting rule, therefore: *More numbers than a single small group? Show them visually!*

Some audiences include highly numerate executives with computer-type minds. They crunch numbers like others eat peanuts, and can hardly be fed too many. Each number must then be meticulously correct. They have their calculators out (or can do sums at lightning speed in their heads) to check and possibly query or correct you. Don't leave figures on view too long. It tempts nit-pickers.

At the other extreme are many valuable human beings who still count on their fingers, often using only one hand. Not long ago, the Government's Assessment of Performance Unit revealed that one in five children leaves school incapable of arranging whole numbers in order of size. That is nothing new. Lord Randolph Churchill (Winston's father) grumbled about decimals: 'I could never make out what they meant with those damned dots.' He was, at the time, Chancellor of the Exchequer.

The aim, when presenting statistics, should therefore be to leave your audience with ideas that are easy to remember. Simple aims, like 'Beating the million' or Sir Roger Bannister's historic cracking the four-minute-mile are best. Low-number ratios, like the famous 'One in three is not using Amplex' are easiest to retain mentally.

Four simple rules for presenting figures must begin with (Rule 1): Don't put too many on one visual. A list of, say, 14 headings on a flipchart, slide or transparency, with four columns of figures to read across against each, makes 70 facts for the eye to explore. These are not visual aids, but visual confusers. Yet presenters often show them.

In Amsterdam, I sat through a gruelling day of computer print-outs converted into projected 'numerical wallpaper'. Presenters waved a carefree hand towards the screen, glibly exclaiming 'As you can readily see. . . .' All experts—even they confounded each other.

If figures are to be presented in mass, a vital few must be picked out with a ring of colour, a pointer accurately directed, or other device, to be talked about in detail. The function of the rest is then to impress rather than inform.

Rule 2 is to stay with one method of representing information, not mix them. 'More than one-third lacked a bath in 1952,' wrote a newspaper economist. 'Twenty-five years later, 91 in 100 boasted their own bath.' Confusing. From 1952 to 1977, homes with baths rose from under 66 to over 90 per cent. Why not say so?

Figures mean little unless (Rule 3) we have a comparison base to give them perspective. This was indeed supplied by the journalist writing about baths, above. Figures gain meaning if we know comparable ones about other times, places, factors, companies, or countries.

Rule 4 is to represent the numbers, if you can, as diagrams, especially for less numerate or larger audiences.

The pie chart is ideal for showing proportions of a total devoted to different purposes. From an early age, anyone brought up in a family of children develops an acute eye for the angle of cake or pie he or she is apportioned by Mother, compared with others.

Bar charts fit into slides (though not flipcharts) more readily when horizontal. We read this way, left to right. And annotations are easier to decipher when horizontal.

Graphs are a common language, ideal for showing varying results through time. Different colours of line will not show at any distance, unless thickly marked, but are useful when they do.

Symbols, in my opinion, can be overdone. Squads of buses or

bananas in regimented rows, lines of cans or cartons—these may amuse kids. They are insulting to adults. Use with discretion.

Because they tend to appear convincing and unanswerable, and so have been used unscrupulously to confuse and mislead, figures tend to have a reputation that arouses cynicism. 'Lies, damn lies, and statistics,' people quote. 'Statistics,' wrote the humorist, Lionel Strachey, 'are mendacious truths.'

'You cannot feed the hungry on statistics,' cried Lloyd George. But you cannot feed them today without, so the good presenter uses them clearly and sincerely. He backs them up *after* the presentation with a report where they are given in detail.

Films. How to introduce them effectively into presentations

Making films (as distinct from using them) is a specialism outside the scope of this book. But showing a film in a presentation— your own, or one you hire or buy—is something every presenter should understand. Rightly done, it can shine like the stained glass in Coventry Cathedral.

Don't just put it into the run of the presentation, leaving it to look after itself. People easily go off into their own fantasy when watching a film and can miss the point entirely.

Tell the audience briskly and vividly what the film shows, how it fits into the theme of your presentation, and *what you want them to see*. This directing of attention is vital. It concentrates their minds on what is important, especially if it is announced that someone will comment on it afterwards, expecting them to join in the discussion.

What film cannot do is to accommodate to the audience. It won't answer questions. Heckling won't stop it. If people start laughing and talking, or leave in a body, it grinds blandly on.

49

The best film in the world cannot replace the human being, the flesh and blood, the voice and smile. This is why popes, presidents and princes go walkabouts with crowds and why you—the presenter—must maintain initiative over your film.

Flipchart arts. Making your mark with pad and felt pen

You can make a mess or a masterpiece on this large pad of white paper, usually hung from the top of a suitable easel, with a ledge for markers. It is an honest working tool for a straight occasion. A big advantage is that it contains few technical hazards—no switches, bulbs, fuses, lenses, screen, or power supply to go wrong.

Your use of a flipchart can be as sophisticated as a Picasso etching or as primitive as graffiti on a wall, according to your wish, your skill, and the requirements of the occasion. There are three main techniques. You can slash onto blank sheets as you make your presentation; turn pages of visuals carefully prepared in advance; or mix the two methods.

1. Precautions before you begin your brilliant instant while-they-watch visuals: stand the easel where everyone can see it: make sure the paper is secure and won't avalanche down; check that the markers are well charged with ink, not dry or about to fade out.

If you are a creative genius, you need no more preparation. If you are not, do a fast miniature dummy run on a postcard-size pad as a rehearsal. This will allow you to visualize the layout and (being small) will restrain you from overcrowding it.

Plan your colours—two are usually enough (red and blue or black), three are plenty.

Prepare the actual flipchart sheets with faint horizontal and vertical guide lines in pencil, three to six inches apart. Similarly, pencil in the main outline of any difficult graph, diagram, or drawing. The pencil lines will be invisible to the audience but will guide your 'instant' drawing or lettering.

Restrict each piece to laconic simplicity, keeping your back to the audience only for the briefest seconds. Nothing is so boring as the back view of a presenter mumbling sentences to himself as he writes them in full on the wall. Interrupt anything that is too long by turning back to the audience momentarily with a remark.

Don't leave the visual up when you have finished with it. Step in front of it to obscure it temporarily, or flip it over the top of the easel out of the way. If you rip it off, make sure in advance that you can tear it without collapsing the easel.

Unless you enjoy working up to your knees in autumn leaves, or intend to stick the used sheets around the walls as a gallery of notes, have a large carton or waste-basket for discarded sheets.

2. Preparing in advance, you can lay the flipchart flat or on a draughtsman's sloping desk and work more easily. A slip-under sheet marked boldly with horizontals and verticals will ensure your pencilled layout does not stagger, droop, or run uphill.

In a pre-prepared flipchart sequence, there should be more opportunity for the pictorial or diagrammatic as opposed to the merely verbal. A sketch of the product is tremendously worth while.

Keep in mind that people probably have to read your figures, words, and pictures from 30 to 40 feet away, or more. Test the letter-height by looking at it from that distance. Print large, with not much on a sheet. It's a visual, not a report.

If your lettering (and spelling) are good enough to match the importance of the presentation, finish the work. An amateur artist will probably get a more dashing effect by doing it quickly. Amateurism looks most amateur when it is painstaking. Illegible calligraphers should recruit help from a professional artist or talented friend.

When your lettering or drawing is done in advance, use alternate sheets, with blanks between, so as to enable you to discard one visual without uncovering the next till you are ready. This will also avoid see-through from one to the next (which distracts

51

inquisitive audiences) and give you some extra scribbling space if wanted.

3. On a prepared visual, you can still leave certain portions merely pencilled in—graphs, totals, percentages. Then, at the moment of presentation, dash them in dramatically with your felt marker.

You can also reveal to the audience parts of the flipchart that are prepared by having them folded up from the bottom, and stapled through at the edge. Some 'Hey presto!' technique as you rip it into view will add drama.

Delivering from a prepared flipchart, stand beside it with your chest no nearer the audience than is the paper. Then you can't obscure it by accident.

Don't talk in different words from the wording you show. Announce the same heading as charted. Then talk on from there. Otherwise the eyes and the ears of the audience receive different messages and you make communication difficult.

The final advantage of the flipchart is that its basics—a few sheets rolled up, a felt marker or two, and a couple of large bulldog clips—are probably more easily and safely portable than any other simple visual system.

PS: Check through your sheets immediately before presenting. Jokers who annotate a sheet with extra or naughty words can throw you badly.

G

Gaffe, clanger, *faux pas*, aberration—what should you do?

Once in every presenter's lifetime comes the awful moment when he opens his mouth and puts his foot in it. Dr William Spooner, warden of New College, Oxford, proposing the Loyal Toast to the Queen was alleged to have said: 'Let us drink to the queer old Dean'.

Mix-ups of the tongue frequently arise from fatigue. Unconscious aggression against the client, the boss, or a colleague may be a deeper cause. What can you do to prevent such slips? Resentments are best thoroughly aired in advance privately and come to terms with. Scripts should be read out loud to discover and remove any incipient tongue-trippers.

If you nevertheless drop a clanger, make as little fuss about it as possible. One immediate and sincere public correction may be necessary. But don't dwell on it. A subsequent tactful word of contrition to the injured person should be made at the earliest moment, privately.

News broadcasters and commentators sometimes do not even put themselves right. 'Never apologize,' said Brian Johnston, the cricket commentator who calls himself the Chief Gaffer, mentioning some of his own funnier slips. 'Just go on and people think it hasn't happened'.

Gestures that illustrate and emphasize your sell

Conscious gesture is well understood by audiences in its broader forms. Yorkshire horseman Harvey Smith went into the dictionaries of slang when he raised a two-fingered 'victory sign' on winning at a horse show.

I am not recommending such strong sign-language as that. But in some business circles it has become the correct presentation style to remain almost immobile—an invisible psychic armour adopted, I believe, to avoid betraying fear.

Gesture, movement, facial expression (even if politely muted) are part of a universal vocabulary, and we de-humanize and handicap ourselves by failing to use it. The golden rule of gesture is action first, words after. This is the most impactful way.

If a display crashes down, a gesture of mock despair as you clutch your head breaks the tension for the audience. We can accuse, like politicians, by pointing a finger at a wrong idea. Or, we can convey determination by clenching a fist.

Presenting in English to audiences from foreign countries, I find that occasional mime helps to improve understanding of some facts and situations. They can read the gesture quicker than understanding the words.

There is no need to ham it up. But when useful optimistic enthusiasm is there to be expressed, it is wasteful to restrain it.

With the notable exception of the arm-waving wonderman, Professor Magnus Pyke, the influence of TV performance has toned down the gestures of performers today. Finger-wagging and stabbing are out. So is chopping or sawing the air. And books about oratory no longer illustrate their pages, as in Victorian times, with a semaphoring speaker looking like Kali, the multi-armed Hindu goddess.

Nevertheless, 'He who uses no gestures looks like a constipated prig,' said *Punch* magazine recently, in a page of satirical fun, which nevertheless contained much good sense. 'Pounding the

54

rostrum will merely spill water and send shock-waves through the microphones, stunning the audience,' it said, 'but go ahead if it makes you feel better.'

Gifts, reports, souvenirs, samples, and hand-outs—when?

The new forward planning executive of an international food company was preparing his first presentation to the board of directors. The company secretary asked him for copies of his back-up document for distribution, as usual, in advance. 'Sorry, no reports until afterwards,' said the new man firmly. After a tussle, the company's precedent of years was set aside. To the mild surprise of eight directors, the presentation went ahead purely on voice and visuals. The documentation followed after. It worked well.

Exactly at what moment you distribute your gifts, samples, souvenirs, reports, documents, and visuals can make or mar the presentation.

A lady presenting the new season's fabrics to representatives from the big London retail stores was asked if she had samples. Unthinkingly, she handed a few to people in the front row, who passed them on and reached out for more. In a few moments, the audience of 30 men and women were all examining pieces of cloth and ignoring the speaker. If you want your audience to stay with you and listen, don't give them any excuse to turn elsewhere. Show your patterns, by all means, if they are (as with the fabric lady) a vital part of the presentation. But better still to show them as colour slides where you have control, and can switch them on and off at will.

Show the figures that the directors will find in your report, but as visuals first, and on paper only when you have finished.

Even with a visual too small for a whole audience to see at once, don't be tempted to pass it round. It rips a circulating section out of your listeners' attention. Pass it round after you finish speaking.

If you have gifts, samples, or souvenirs certainly describe, illustrate, and promise them during your presentation. But give them out as your final act.

Grammatical English. Unfortunate impact of promotion stoppers

A vigorous young Englishman worked as financial controller overseas for a large British company. They wanted to make him a director. But although he held high accountancy qualifications, his English was suspect. In presenting figures he was likely to bring out such solecisms as 'you was' or 'I done it'. Promotion stoppers! His chief executive, a well-educated man, would not countenance them.

Habitual errors in speech by ambitious men are often stubborn. Such chaps become successful through their strong personality. It sometimes makes them resist all attempts to 'improve' their grammar. They fear their personality being tampered with or are fiercely loyal to the speech patterns of their parents, family, friends, or neighbourhood.

The best approach is to suggest that they learn a special second language—presenter's English for presentations, just as they might learn French for France. The wish to change must come from within. My accountant friend was willing to spend three days of his holiday at a remote country hotel cooperating in a total immersion consultation about his communication skills. He flew back overseas with a suitcase of books to study.

The great difficulty in presenting grammatically is that the

56

English language continually moves and grows. Especially in advertising agencies, where the young poets and writers of commerce reside, presenters often pioneer new usage. They have nevertheless a responsibility for maintaining the beauty, purity, and strength of the Queen's English to the best of their ability, as have all presenters.

You need to present in fresh, vivid language appropriate to your subject. It is good business, also, to keep in touch with the grammatical nuances of client terminology. Pay tactful attention to 'Client's Grammar' which may have idiosyncracies to observe or avoid.

The successful presenter levels with the grammar of his audience. When the 'you was' accountant revisted Britain a year later, his grammar was completely boardroom. Within a week, they made him a finance director.

H

Hands. What to do with them usefully when presenting

Your hands should be an asset in communication. Imagine, for instance, an Italian trying to explain something with his hands tied behind his back. He would be speechless. Yet from English delegates the most frequent question I get is 'What shall I do with my hands?'

Doctors agree that our dominant hand and the speech centres of our brain are connected through the autonomous nervous system. So, if you grasp your hands behind your back, or get rid of them in some other way, you are handicapping your self-expression.

Allow yourself something appropriate to hold if you wish. Avoid repetitive hand mannerisms. But realize that as you travel the world, hand gesture is a language almost universally understood.

> Hands uncontrolled your nervousness betray.
> Avoid your pockets and your cash or keys.
> Notes held in hand will help you on your way.
> Don't let your fingers fidget, speaker, please.
> Spontaneous gesture clinches what you say.

Too many English presenters allow their arms and hands to hang like straight sticks. Italians keep their arms comfortably bent at the elbow, as if ready to gesture. Try it.

Heckling. How to deal with it—and keep the client

A canvassing councillor stood in an open Land Rover, shouting a political speech through a loud-hailer at the home-going crowds in a busy London street. They hurried by without a glance. Then a little man shuffled along the gutter. 'Rubbish!' he screeched. 'Why don't you go 'ome?' In moments people gathered and the speaker had an audience.

My friend John Winkler, business author and international business lecturer, quotes this personal experience as evidence that presenters should not fear but welcome heckling. Of course, there is a considerable difference between politics and presentation. But one good heckle can undoubtedly set an audience alight.

The problem for novice speakers is knowing how to control heckling. You must not ignore interruptions. It is easy to be deflated, or at the other extreme to be too rude. Any fool can win an argument and lose an audience.

Aneurin Bevan was once asked a question, quite politely, which annoyed him. 'Young woman,' he said, 'if you will keep quiet I will educate you—and you need education.' A chill came over the audience. They didn't like his unfairness.

An earlier politician so enraged a gathering in Birmingham Town Hall he had to be smuggled out of the back doors, disguised as one of a squad of policemen. His life was in danger.

Only when the audience is thoroughly on the presenter's side and wishes the interrupter would shut up can the speaker squash him. 'Temper, temper,' an audience chanted at Edward Heath, after he snapped at a heckler. He saved the situation with a broad grin.

Stratford Johns, the actor, was continually heckled in a London theatre by a man in the front of the circle. 'What a load of rubbish,' said the play-goer loudly. 'What a boring play!' People asked him to be quiet, but he kept on.

Finally, the actor turned on him and said: 'Look, if you don't like it, why don't you shut up and go home? I'll refund you the price of your ticket.' The audience cheered and the man didn't say another word.

Prince Philip had similar trouble with a student at Edinburgh University. 'Shut up and grow up,' rapped Philip and the rest clapped.

Everyone has thought of the brilliant response after the meeting is over. Don't fret that it is too late. You are sharpening up for the next time when you will be better able to get a laugh and win the exchange.

Avoid rhetorical questions. Hecklers snap them up like early birds swallowing worms. 'What is it that is responsible for the wonderful rising birthrate under the Socialist Government?' asked a Labour speaker. Voice at the back of the hall: 'Private enterprise!'

Two centuries ago, Lord Sandwich started a famous exchange by hurling at a speaker: 'You will either die on the scaffold or of venereal disease'.

'That depends, my lord,' came the stinging answer, 'whether I embrace your principles or your mistress'.

Unless you are quelling an unruly conference of salesmen, or something similar, the task for a presenter is to accept heckling with good humour and gratitude as something that livens up the meeting. Above all, smile and keep your temper. Certainly don't argue. Your first priority is to keep a worthwhile client. 'A soft answer turneth away wrath,' says the wise old *Book of Proverbs*. 'But grievous words stir up anger'.

Hostility in presentation audiences and how to defuse it

I was invited by a managing director to make a presentation to a dozen of his managers in Lancaster. For some reason they resented it and unfortunately the MD was elsewhere when I arrived. 'Before you start,' said one burly executive, rising to his feet, 'I'm the general manager of this place, and I need this presentation like a hole in the head.' He said his secretary would come in with an empty envelope in half an hour. He would use that as an excuse to leave—unless the thing was good. Two others said likewise.

'Thank you, gentlemen, for your warm Northern welcome,' I replied, smiling. 'Let's get on.'

Hostility in meetings can arise from unexpected causes. A director of a London advertising agency asked me to prepare an extra lecture for a training course, on 'How to Deal with Hostile Audiences'. I remarked about it to another executive. 'Oh dear old Jack always has touchy meetings,' he said. 'He just has this gift for brushing people up the wrong way.'

Whatever its cause, you can often feel hostility before you see it. The emotional atmosphere is cold. People are uncooperative and negative: they exchange the small normal pleasantries stiffly and grudgingly.

The hostile person sighs as if suffering too much. Clicks his tongue. Hisses to himself. Taps and fidgets. Glares about, mutters to himself, and perhaps tries to involve his neighbour. He may shake his head, look disbelievingly astonished, and even laugh contemptuously. Alternatively, he may withdraw emotionally by taking no notice, looking away, reading ostentatiously, or otherwise detaching himself—or he may actually withdraw physically by leaving the meeting.

In most instances, the majority of people welcome anything that warms an icy atmosphere and lessens tension. They find cold meetings uncomfortable, and fear a row which is perhaps not of their making. After a disagreement or a sharp exchange, they often take time to thaw and relax.

Comfortable surroundings, reasonable warmth and lighting, and a hospitable atmosphere tend to lessen hostility. But more important is the emotional attitude of the presenter. Sometimes it helps to break off, adjourn, have a drink, and let tempers cool.

It is important not to get angry, scold, quarrel, or vilify. By all means take matters seriously and listen courteously to criticism. Be stern if necessary, but calm.

Sometimes a bit of ritual loud-talk and table thumping has to be allowed to certain people. They can then go away boasting 'I told him a thing or two'. But biting the tongue and not making acid responses is better than saying unforgivable things that can't later be unsaid.

Establishing friendly relationships is not a passive matter of avoiding displeasing. Picking out the hostile person for kindly reference, making much of him, deferring to him, asking him to contribute, not allowing him to sulk, pleasantly making him a person of importance—these are devices hard to withstand.

My hole-in-the-head man at Lancaster became a staunch friend. 'When you lasted the first hour,' he said, 'we thought you were doing well.' The girl who brought in his empty envelope was puzzled by the gust of laughter that greeted her.

Humour. Should it be used in your presentations? A touchy question

'Should I try to introduce humour into my presentations?' Inside many a serious, profit-orientated boss, it seems, there is a laugh-hungry funster eager for applause. Humour is a useful lubricant for communication, but can backfire or fizzle. What are the parameters?

1. If you are a prosperous Mr Sober-Sides in everyday life, don't attempt to emulate a top comedian in one convulsive leap on an important business occasion. Ten-to-one you'll die. For those who wish to cavort in the exhilarating waters of humour, the place to begin is the shallow end. Practice with colleagues, family, and friends on social and light business occasions or in the non-risk environment of a presentation course.

2. Never do a tryout on anyone who may pinch your story and use it publicly before you can. You can't trust your best friend over this and certainly not your boss, who is probably well accustomed to appropriating your ideas. Don't rehearse either to cynical subordinates, a humourless secretary, or an impatient wife. Their reactions may deflate you.

3. Realize that using humour effectively is the most difficult of speaking skills. It requires first the most careful selection and marshalling of your material. The background facts must be sketched economically and in the right order.

Humour can be made or marred by the vocal intonation—the varying pitch of the voice. The word 'handbag', for instance, is not normally a riotous rib-tickler. But a good actress will do marvellous things with it in Oscar Wilde's play, *The Importance of Being Earnest*. A man admits to having been a foundling in a handbag on a railway station. 'A handbag?' cries the imperious lady. Collapse of audience.

Finally, the timing and emphasis on the punch line must be confident and should unmistakably signal for the audience to laugh.

4. You must take special care what subject you select for making fun. The wrong topic can blast you sky high. Obviously dangerous (except for experts) are all the normal booby-traps: race, colour, religion, politics, and blue stories. So are illnesses, operations, and funerals.

The hazard increases with a tiny audience at presentations, consisting of very important people. Someone's sensibilities may easily be upset by unhappy personal coincidence. A harmless husband-wife joke can become terribly embarrassing, for instance, if someone present is newly bereaved.

Humour should come easily and naturally from the speaker's personality and his subject. An unfunny man telling a joke that does not integrate with his main subject is usually a calamity.

5. Be reassured, however, that smart quips which fly like shooting

64

stars are not outside the bounds of possibility. One happy day you'll startle yourself when a fast witticism issues unbidden from your lips. 'Hi!' you'll think, as the audience rocks with mirth. 'Did I say that?'

6. But pause and consider. Do you truly want to win laughs? If you've the reputation of being a comedian, you can get badly stuck with it so that superiors refuse to take you seriously.

Top men and women seldom, if ever, try to be publicly funny. Queen Elizabeth the First, Oliver Cromwell, Charles De Gaulle, and other greats didn't make cracks—only history. The exception was President Abraham Lincoln who, alas, was assassinated.

The final point is that audiences must be mentally ready for humour, or they won't take it. Unless you are very confident, it is possibly better to concentrate on cheerfulness, optimism, briskness, enthusiasm, and smiles. Humour is not always acceptable in the serious aspects of business.

Hypo-glycaemia. When it hits and what action to take

Hypo-glycaemia is a medical expression I first heard from a research man at Cadbury-Schweppes, in St Albans, Hertfordshire. I am no doctor, but understand it means deficiency of sugar in the blood, which can be a sore handicap to presenters.

After a good lunch, with plentiful alcoholic refreshment, the body over-compensates for the excess fuel by burning it up faster. Result: around four o'clock, hypo-glycaemia is high and attention low. This is the fatal hour when presenters falter and the client yawns. If you put him in the dark for slides or a film, he almost inevitably nods.

Improved ventilation is one aid to wakefulness. The tea interval saves everyone's honour. Don't serve teacups to people sitting down. Get them onto their feet and preferably walking through to a refreshment lobby. Serve them refills. Also, let there be sweet biscuits—the blood is calling for energy fuel.

I

Impromptu speaking. Instant brilliance when you know nothing about it

Crisis! You have to make a brilliant speech at a moment's notice on a subject about which you know almost nothing. An American wit had the answer. He said: 'It usually takes me three weeks to prepare a good impromptu speech.'

Three simple things will steer you successfully through this ordeal:

A. A full mind.

B. A ready attitude of mind.

C. A standardized fallback procedure.

A. Discussing the qualifications for the higher ranges of entrepreneurship, Nigel Broackes, chairman of Trafalgar House, also defined the full mind that is needed for success in impromptu speaking: '. . . a spectrum of information far broader than the boundaries of the business itself'. The way to this qualification is regular reading of newspapers, books, and periodicals, through meeting people, and from radio and TV. 'It is a form of self-education that cannot be learned at school, and should start as soon as one left.' He might well have added that it is a lifelong job.

B. The right attitude of mind is readiness to have a go.

Impromptu success takes time. 'It comes as a complete surprise to me to be addressing you here. . . .'

Impromptu is a Latin-rooted term (similar to prompt) signifying 'in readiness'.

C. What appals novice impromptu performers is the feeling of having nothing to say. That is the moment for having recourse to the easy steps of our fallback formula. You can tick it off on the five digits of one hand.

1. *Begin deliberately, thoughtfully, and on a postive note.* Don't set too fast a pace. You are delivering a small speech, not an epigram. Give yourself time to think. The person who goes off like a rocket falls down like the stick.

And positive? It means being hopeful, optimistic, and forward looking. Your impromptu speech will come to a premature end if you allow negative thoughts to enter your mind.

2. *Lay out some thoughts and ideas, aloud.* If you were scribbling a short speech, you'd note down some notions. Now you can only do this out loud. Survey possibilities quickly and skim around the probable outline.

3. *Now choose one main line, and say what it is.* It's unwise to try to make more than one point in a short impromptu. Pick one, make it clear which you've picked, and expand on it.

4. *Back up your main contention with evidence.* Once having settled upon a point, weak speakers tend to fizzle out. To give weight to your remarks, draw upon your full mind, mentioned above. A case history, a quote from some authority, a simple statistic, even an incident or recent experience—something of this kind, especially if first-hand or authoritative, will give specific impact to what otherwise would probably be a generalization. You will feel more confident once you have brought in some evidence of this kind.

5. *Finally, sum up strongly.* If you want to make an impact with your impromptu (and not just fade gently out of the scene) forget how tentatively you may have begun, and finish on a clear confident note. You can say: 'What is it I want to leave with you on this point? What should we remember? It is . . . .' Look back over what you have said, and reiterate the main point succinctly and in brief memorable words. You have finished successfully. You have made an effective impromptu speech.

Never dodge the call to make an impromptu speech. The boss

who shoves you in at the deep end is doing you a good turn, providing you survive. The reason for this is that there is a secondary bonus. Prepared speeches are sweated over and rehearsed in advance—often a long and painful job. But impromptu speeches are delivered without preparation, then rehearsed *afterwards*. You can't help going over what you said again and again. Each time you are teaching yourself more about speaking and presentation.

Interruptions. How to cope with them—and win

Fifty student first-aiders were teamed into pairs in a hotel conference room. One of each team had, as instructed, securely splinted both legs of the recumbent partner for double compound fractures (pretended). Then—not for practice, but for a real emergency—the fire alarm rang and everyone had to get out quickly.

Some interruptions at presentations should be foreseen. Traffic and aircraft noise can be expected if the only ventilation is open windows. Playtime in the schoolyard next door will produce 15 minutes of yelling pandemonium. It is probably best to give way to temporary interruptions, take a break, and perhaps actually enjoy them. Even top directors enjoy watching fire engines or a bannered protest march.

Hammering on the next floor, high jinks among noisy staff, or darts thudding into your partition wall can be silenced, as a rule, by an urgent message to the management. Don't go yourself, especially if you are an unknown. You may get a rude answer. Most frequent interruption in presentation rooms is the telephone. It should be removed and calls intercepted elsewhere.

At a presentation to the Publicity Association of Brighton and

Sussex, I was interrupted by a large dog pushing open swing doors, crossing the room, and shouldering out through another pair the other side. When the smiling audience had finally settled, the dog did the reverse trip. No wonder actors fear working with animals! All you can do is to let the laughter die down. Make a pleasantry, recapitulate to the point at which you were interrupted, and then proceed as before.

J

Jargon. Don't high-hat audiences with incomprehensibilities

After an intense 10-minute presentation from a young marketing man, a senior executive said: 'Not wishing to be unkind, I must say I hardly understood a word of that. I don't think anyone else did, either. Can we have it in simpler language, please?'

What is meaningful specialist language to those deeply steeped in a technicality is often meaningless jargon to those outside—like talking Icelandic to a Bantu. There are four reasons presenters use it, but only one is completely acceptable.

First, they talk in jargon because they can't help it. Some stiff minds become so soaked in the technical way of thinking that they are totally unable to talk in everyday terms. 'He is the brains of General Motors,' it was said of one ideas man, 'but doesn't speak any known language.'

Second, they speak in jargon because they want to maintain the mystery in order to protect their status. 'Oedematous . . .' murmurs the doctor, feeling your twisted ankle. He means swollen. Well, a certain amount of mystery may make us more suggestible to cure and to that extent is justified. But jargon also is a put-down for those who don't understand it. At the extreme, it is insulting and you can lose clients by using it.

Third, presenters who are not as knowledgeable as they would wish often use jargon to impress others. If the audience 'wonk a tib' (Cockney back-slang jargon for 'know a bit') it tells them that the presenter is masquerading as more expert than he actually is.

Fourth, the acceptable use of jargon is to introduce essential terms tactfully so that the uninitiated feel that they, too, begin to be in the know. This makes the client a member of the club, and helps cement good relationship. Top men, especially, are fond of blunt down-to-earth terms. So jargon must only be employed, like spice, according to taste.

The jargon of which to be most wary is the word with a generally accepted common meaning which the presenter is likely to employ, confusingly to laymen, in some special abstruse way. 'Breadboard' in electronic research and development, for instance, means a board carrying a trial hook-up circuit, not something on which to slice a loaf.

Jokes about clients. Are they ever safe?

While the editor of a national magazine was briefing me one morning in my journalistic days, he offered me coffee. 'If you're having some, yes please,' I said.

It came in a cracked cup with a non-matching saucer—nothing remarkable in editorial offices. But then they brought in the editor's. His cup was almost the size of grandmother's antique washbasin, all glorious in scarlet and gold, its saucer nearly as big as a dustbin lid.

I kept a straight face until it was time to go. Then I expressed thanks for the refreshment, and added laughing; 'Mind you don't fall in that thing. You'll drown yourself.'

Is it wise to laugh at customers and clients? A marketing manager of an international company had what was obviously a three-part Dutch surname. 'I must get the spelling right. It's a little difficult,' smiled a caller.

'It's a perfectly good old English name,' said the marketing man stiffly and ended the business relationship from that moment.

Most businessmen can laugh at themselves a little, providing they make the joke. But nearly all hate looking foolish and defacing their dignity. With notable exceptions, the really important people have no sense of humour. They didn't get where they are by taking life lightly.

On the other hand, the laughing man has perspective, and so lacks the fanaticism that could drive him to the top. He reaches middle management. You can safely rib him a little.

In presentations, however, jokes are dynamite that can blow you sky high. Handle with care. Make them only about safe topics: yourself, competitors, taxation, or the client's favourite 'whipping boy'.

The John May commandment about humour in presentation will probably offend someone, though it is serious enough:

> Thou shalt not laugh at thy client's company names
> Thou shalt not laugh at thy client's business aims
> Nor at his product lines
> Nor at his logo signs
> Nor his fads
> Nor his ads
> Nor at anything that this thy client's is
> Or appertaineth in any way to his biz.

The same goes for his own name, physical characteristics, baldness, wig, eccentric habits, car, home, hobbies, or what have you. 'Love me, love my dog' is a precept so old and wise that it was originally Latin. I never wrote for that magazine again.

Knowing your subject utterly. Have yourself pre-grilled

The flag that makes you free in presentation is complete knowledge of your subject. It is not a standard you achieve merely by study. You need a devil's advocate to fight you fit.

To prepare for tough press questions at its annual general meeting, a computer company assembled its directors for a grilling. Two of the most aggressive and knowledgeable managers bombarded them with a prolonged session of awkward questions. Answers were pruned, polished, and made publicly presentable. 'After that,' they told me, 'the press conference was a doddle.'

John Kennedy, preparing himself for the famous TV confrontation with Richard Nixon, spent three days being grilled by his aides. Then he threw down his papers. 'I'm ready for him,' he said.

For TV interviews, Lord Thomson of Fleet, then proprietor of *The Sunday Times* and *The Times*, took considerable trouble. Even TV critics said how relaxed he was when facing the provocative Randolph Churchill. Again, Thomson had been pre-grilled by colleagues, and worked on his answers. 'A good performance,' he said, 'doesn't come by chance.'

Use this technique with CCTV recording your performance against tough interrogation and you can see for yourself on the replay how well you come across.

L

Language quirks that distort the limey-yankee axis

When a presentation transmutes into *pree*-sentation, meaning that American as well as British business persons are present, then comes the time to recall Irish-born dramatist George Bernard Shaw's perceptive quip: 'England and America are two countries separated by the same language.'

In Britain, when you're 'through' on the telephone, you are connected to the other person. Getting through to an audience means being understood. But the American who is through is finished.

At a Geneva Disarmament Conference, American and British delegates fell out over two meanings of *tabling* an action. When a US company was negotiating with the UK's giant Imperial Chemical Industries, a like misunderstanding arose. To the British, tabling a matter means putting it down for discussion. To the Americans, the word conveys shelving (deferring) it indefinitely.

British presenters in America can easily commit solecisms that shock in respectable company. A fag (British bother or cigarette) is a homosexual. 'Knocking someone up' in England means knocking on their door to wake them; in American, to make them pregnant.

79

Such variations must be watched. American units, for instance, are not only different but (like their golfballs) bigger. However, British drinkers can restore their self-conceit by realizing that their famous British pint contains 20 per cent more than the American one.

Lectern, rostrum, table, pulpit. How will they help you?

A car company decided to take the year's convention to Florida as a treat for the dealers. But the hotel was not so well prepared as promised. The rostrum on stage, for instance, consisted of several cardboard boxes, stacked on their sides and draped with baize. Inside the top box was a jug of water and glass for the speakers.

Launching the presentations on the first morning, the dynamic PR man grasped the makeshift rostrum, threw himself enthusiastically back, and accidentally emptied the jug into his trousers. From that moment, the convention was a riotous success.

Many good presenters object to being anchored to one spot by a lectern, rostrum, or table and I think they are right. Audiences like to see as much of you as possible, not just a head and gripping hands like a bus driver. Therefore you should stand, not sit (unless you are chairman) and come into the open if you can.

There are occasions, however, when you have to stay with the rostrum's push-buttons, warning lights, microphone, and script-desk. Even in this situation, it pays sometimes to walk out from behind, and address a few extra words, an aside, or a comment to the audience off the record. Even if you are on a halter microphone, you can still do this. People will feel you are confiding in them and respond more warmly. Anything which comes between you and them is an obstacle to presentation. You don't want barricades, you want communication.

Length of presentations. Words, minutes, and what is ideal

Rugged, eloquent old Lord Brabazon of Tara once said in the House of Lords that any good speaker should be able to make his point in five minutes, maximum.

As life grows more complex, we are less willing to spend much time on anything. The most popular newspapers have the largest type and the shortest articles. The duration of advertisements on television is measured in seconds. So how long should a presentation last?

One of the special characteristics of presentation is that the duration of the performance is often fixed not by the wishes of performers, nor the needs of the subject—the audience fixes the duration according to how long they think they can spare. If there is one certainty about this specified duration, it is that it will not be kept. Probably it will start late; the presenters will be on time, but the complete audience not. It may finish on time, but possibly have its end eroded by unavoidable early departures of top people while underlings play out the charade of seeing it through. Alternatively, a top client may get the bit between his teeth, and elongate it by hours.

The presenters must be above reproach in their time-keeping, quick on their feet, ready to edit shorter with brilliant effect, or even to recapitulate a section because of a late important arrival. If they run short of time, gabbling won't help. They must cut. They are not in the strong position of comedian 'Professor' Jimmy Edwards in Detroit, when told he was talking too fast. 'Then *think* faster!' he roared.

Right from the first conception, presenters must be conscious of what the available time will allow them to say lucidly and persuasively. Many presenters, I find, are frightened that they won't have enough to say. Then in rehearsal they over-run by up to 100 per cent. Cutting from this dimension means a rewrite.

It is safe practice to set out to fill three-quarters of your time.

Presentations always grow longer. Points have to be explained. Little bits of humour come in. Inspiration seizes you.

Two practical tips will help.

1. If I have to prepare a half-hour presentation, I write 3000 words, or 100 words for each minute of duration. People easily speak to an audience half as fast again as this. But the margin is taken up by exposition, recapitulation, bringing in visuals, and so on. Ten typewritten lines (100 words) per minute is good rule-of-thumb timing.

2. To help you reach the END on time, the acronym's initials can be used for marking paragraphs for inclusion or omission, according to time's dictates: E for *Essential*, not to be omitted whatever happens; N for *Necessary*, to be kept in normally, but deleted in a crisis; D for *Desirable*, or good for use, if possible. If all the presentation team practises these disciplines efficiently, you should win inside the time limit.

Lighting the way to a shining presentation

To ensure a bright and shining presentation, you must find time to make certain dull checks. When you visit the venue in advance, find out where the light switches are and try them. Which operate on which lights? Are all the lights working? Nothing is so dismal and disreputable as a dead panel or bulb. If there is a dud, get it replaced, even at the cost of a fuss.

Despite daylight, most presentation, conference, and meeting rooms look more cheerful with the lights on. In thunderstorms, rainy days, early winter evenings, or eclipses, artificial lighting is essential.

The audience needs to be able to see the stage, the visuals, and the presenter. Check the visuals to avoid shadowing and to see that dazzling reflections don't hit the audience.

Check that the presenter will have plenty of light to see his notes, documents, and visuals clearly. Ensure that he is not blinded by lights, positioned too low, shining up into his eyes.

Check finally that strong light does not fall on the screen, dimming slides, films, or overhead projection. Switch off the offending candelabra or shut out the sunshine with a curtain.

A floodlight on the presenter (two at most) helps with making video recordings. The room may need to be dimmed for playback on the monitor.

Some shy presenters welcome darkness for slide sequences. But they lose audience contact by being merely a voice in darkness. Ideally, a soft limelight should illuminate the presenter, and a good reading light play on his notes or script.

For more intricate lighting tricks than these call in an expert. But remember that illumination is all. As the psychologist, Carl Jung, said of human existence, so with presentation: 'The sole purpose . . . is to kindle a light.'

Listen and win. When it pays presenters to hold their tongues

The tall, quiet, smiling man who was conducting the presentation slipped the gold signet ring from his finger, setting it thoughtfully on the table before him. The client boss went on talking, sometimes joined by his associates. But previously vociferous presenters only asked agreeable questions, smiled, and nodded. 'It was more than anyone's job was worth, in my team, to interrupt while that ring was on the table,' John Bittleston told me. 'It was our recognized signal that the client should talk.'

Too many presenters are so intent on putting their own case

83

that they forget that communication works two ways. They miss tremendous opportunities to keep their mouths shut and open their minds.

John Bittleston is now managing director of Cerebos Pacific Ltd, in Singapore. Of his early days in two of London's biggest advertising agencies, he said: 'It didn't take us long to realize that the most valuable contributor to a presentation was the client himself. Those few clients who are not simply longing to tell you all about their opportunities and problems can easily be induced to do so by being asked.'

Presentations should be flexible enough to allow for the clients to join in. Just letting other people talk can persuade them with little other effort than biting your own tongue. A job applicant, for instance, was kept waiting for his interview. At last the busy director dashed in. 'What would you like to ask?' he smiled. The interviewee suggested that he would like to hear more about the firm. Enthusiastically, the director began talking, and went on talking. After 50 minutes, he summed up: 'Well, you seem to me OK for the job. When can you start?' The applicant had said practically *nothing*. But his listening was masterly.

We have two ears, which we cannot close, and one mouth, which we can. Some see in this the intentions of Providence. Listening intelligently is a neglected art in business. Being over-anxious to please makes presenters loquacious. A salesman can talk himself into a sale and—if he doesn't shut up—out of the other side again.

The wise Swiss have an inscription: '*Sprechen ist silbern, Schweigen ist golden.*' Speech is silver, silence is golden. As the prosperous masters of keeping totally quiet about things, they should know.

M

Magnet board and other build-up visuals for specials

A cloud is lifted off the UK here, sunshine is smacked on there, and the pattern of weather in the British Isles builds up from now to the immediate future. Every night on BBC television, the weather person demonstrates the effective use of magnet board as a visual aid for presenters.

Build-up visuals—flannel board, pin board, magnet board, etc—are useful for presenting standardized information that grows or varies as the speaker goes on.

The structure of a conglomerate, the international ramifications of a company, the various publics of a PR operation, weather forecasts, traffic flow, naval or aerial formations, warehouse movement—all these lend themselves to presentation by building or adapting a standard picture or design.

The assembly job is like solving a jigsaw puzzle or moving chess pieces on a board. Precautions to take against confusion are twofold. Either have only few pieces, or a plentiful supply of a limited choice (like the weather person). Second, have your pieces arranged in well-marshalled stacks to be brought into use in a carefully rehearsed order. Desperate searching for a missing

85

piece destroys both credibility for the audience and confidence for the presenter.

Magnetism holds the pieces in place on magnet board (with a ferrous metal base). Thin plastic pieces will adhere to a glass-smooth surface for similar use. Pin-board pieces plug into the holes. Coarse sandpaper, flock paper, or Velcro backing holds the pieces to the flannel board. The board can be covered in flannel or felt, or even be a makeshift blanket hung over a blackboard or cupboard.

Instead of building up, it is possible to have a visual in existence, waiting to be revealed by progressively removing stick-on pieces. Both methods need to be used with a certain brisk panache, slap, and certainty, or they tend to become boring.

Mannerisms that irritate and distract. How to kill or cure them

The dressy, bow-tied presenter put his hand in his trouser pocket, rhythmically jingling his money as he spoke. He pointed to a visual, then dived back to jingling again. When we told him afterwards, he strenuously denied it. As many speakers are, he was totally unconscious of his fidgeting.

Nit-picking about habits only makes presenters more anxious, and is counter-productive. But when the mannerisms are so distracting that the audience pays more attention to them than the message, they need kill-or-cure treatment. Especially when people begin to count them, you endanger your case. The judge, Sir James Cassels, hated being repeatedly called 'My Lord' in court. 'It gets on my nerves.' His clerk kept score on one anxious barrister. 'How many?' Cassels demanded. 'In ninety minutes,' said the clerk, 'over three hundred!'

Cleverly used, mannerisms can be part of the unique flavour

and personality of a speaker. Some performers make such habits a stock-in-trade—picking fluff self-consciously from the suit, ruffling their hair, elevating eyebrows—they make mannerisms work for them.

Those that work against a presenter's effectiveness can be put in four main groups:

1. *Verbal mannerisms,* such as repeated use of 'in this connection', 'and so on and so forth'. A colleague or instructor can curb these simply by pointing them out.

2. *Voice mannerisms* betray shyness and lack of confidence. Talking downwards to the floor or table, turning away, dropping the pitch and diminishing the volume to fade out at the ends of sentences—these are common ones. Tape recording the presenter's dying falls, and possibly comparing them with some more cheerful conversational episodes, brings home the mannerism to the speaker. Rehearsing dismal bits to a more optimistic sentence melody (again taped and played back) can start improvement.

3. *Semi-animal noise mannerisms*—grunts, sighs, erm-ahs, nervous coughs, and unnecessary laughs. These are the refuge of inarticulate persons who cannot string together suitable words, but are pressed by circumstance to break the silence. Such speakers can be provided with, and drilled in, phrases that cover much of what they need to say—just as telephone girls were once trained to trill out 'I'm sorry you have been tr-r-roubled'. Many glib salesmen are prescripted in this way.

'Err', 'aah', and 'um' are special nuisances. Their true vocal function is to maintain conversational initiative while you stop to think. Your 'errs' prevent other people prematurely butting in. Like hoots from a ship's siren, they keep the way clear for you. But a presentation is not a conversation nor a sea voyage. As the speaker, you normally do not have to fend off interruption. A silent pause raises expectancy and falls more pleasantly on the ear. Concentrated self-monitoring can delete 'ums' from speech.

4. *Physical mannerisms* have numerous sources. Head-tilting, foot-twisting, arm-twining bashfulness are a return under stress to winsome tricks of childhood. Mouth-holding, eye-rubbing, and jaw- and head-stroking are ways of partially hiding the face from the audience. Rearranging papers and objects is a physical translation of attempts to marshal ideas in the mind. Other jiggles and swayings are self-comfort routines.

We don't want a presenter clamped immovable in a pyschological straightjacket. Acceptable movement gives vitality. But irritating mannerisms can be brought to light by showing them to the speaker on videotape action replay.

The final tactic for curing unwanted mannerisms of any kind is to apply psychological conditioning immediately it occurs. Dr Hans Eysenck, Professor of Psychology at London University, described the case of a child totally unable to spell. A positive reward-machine was fixed up. The child was told words and when he spelt one correctly, a light went on. When he got five right, a red light flashed and a favourite sweet came down the chute, to be grabbed and eaten by the speller. Soon he was spelling as well as his classmates.

MAP theory. What audiences tell you by where they sit

Knowing primitive native customs about where men sit in tribal gatherings, said explorer David Attenborough on TV, helped him run BBC meetings. One day, his accountant arrived late and sat opposite instead of next to him. Why? Attenborough looked down the agenda. When the meeting came to a certain item, he said: 'I propose to postpone this, gentlemen, to a later meeting.'

Afterwards his accountant asked: 'How did you know I was going to fight you on that?'

How the audience chooses to arrange itself in a room gives the presenter vital clues about them. This is the basic axiom of May's Audience Positioning (MAP) theory, which totally agrees with David Attenborough's experience. Based on observation on hundreds of occasions, the MAP theory says that if people come in

May's Audience Positioning (MAP) theory says that people take up positions in meetings which give the presenter clues to their characters.

from the end opposite the presenter, those who tend to their right (the presenter's left) are the conservative, supportive, 'Right'-minded members.

In contrast, the non-supportive members, who are not so likely to agree, proceed to their left (the presenter's right). These are the 'sinister' delegates (in the heraldic meaning)—the 'Lefties'. The presentation wrecker, if there is one, will be found here, probably half way along.

A third group are those who position themselves centrally facing the presenter. I call these the Barons. They are reasonably disposed towards a good presenter. But if he as the 'King' is weak, they become impatient and begin taking over. It is no coincidence that the most senior and powerful people usually take up this position.

One other position has considerable nuisance value. The person at the back, often to your right, who will neither sit down and become audience nor go away. Don't be fooled when he says 'I'm just a fly on the wall'. He is 'The Sniper', and will ping off bullets at you unless you make him join the party. Ask him to make a proper contribution and he'll probably leave.

The size of the presentation room makes considerable differences. With 15 to 20 in a crowded low-ceiling room, people become informal, livelier, more emotional, harder to control, though more suggestible. Spread the same number far apart in a tall ballroom and the temperature drops, the pace slows, and increased formality makes control easier.

Close, straight rows of seats on one level in a hall makes inter-communications within the audience difficult, and leaves power in the hands of the presenters.

A semi-circular formation, a V- or a U-shaped seating plan, as in a boardroom, increases inter-communication. It also allows opinions to split the audience into groups with different section leaders.

Block-facing-block arrangements split the audience into 'them' and 'us'. You then have two armies, two teams, government and opposition lined up face-to-face. MAP theory says this will easily become war. Unless you want to fight your clients, sit beside them agreeably on one side of the table, not opposite.

Splitting those likely to form a block, isolating chatterers, and placing persons where they can or cannot see one another can help you control the presentation reaction. If you cannot arrange for them to sit where you want them to, at least apply MAP theory and watch where they sit. It tells you much and forewarned is forearmed.

Marketing. Why it is a pointer to winning in presentation

If you have a marketing turn of mind, you have the basis for being among the best presenters in business. You can ensure people will listen if you set about *marketing* your ideas.

The chief buyer of a mail order company made a speech enthusing about the cathedral city to which he had just moved. The audience's response was lukewarm. Why? Because, as a buyer, his lightest word normally always carried weight. But now he was not buying but selling and he needed to approach his subject from the viewpoint of what the audience was interested in. He hadn't seen it that way.

People respond eagerly if the message can be presented as concerning them. When Edward Gibbon finished the second volume of *The Decline and Fall of the Roman Empire*, he presented a copy to the King's brother. No outstanding scholar, the Prince said: 'Another damned thick square book! Always scribble, scribble, scribble, eh Mr Gibbon?'

Compare this with the way that William Shakespeare, a century before, had proved himself a much better marketing man. He was commissioned to write a play for bearded, untidy, talkative King James, who enjoyed hunting all day and often fell asleep during the evening's entertainment. Shakespeare created a made-to-measure melodrama, *Macbeth*, to keep James awake.

91

The King had written a book about witches; Shakespeare started the play with witches. James was descended from Kings of Scotland; Shakespeare brought in one of his kingly ancestors, Duncan, and had him murdered in the play. James did not nod off this time. He sat enthralled by every vivid line till the end—when Macduff reappears carrying Macbeth's severed head, and crying 'Hail, King of Scotland!'

Self-interest is the ear-bender. Every businessman knows this. But when he begins presenting, he is often so wrapped up in his own wishes, production, products, and prices that he forgets to look at them from the angle that works in presentations—the client audience's point of view.

The marketing approach is not the sole secret of speaking and presentation success. But marketing-oriented thinking is an important factor in getting audiences to *listen*.

Microphones. How to employ them effectively in large presentations

Lord Feather told this story against himself. Addressing a large meeting, he asked: 'Can you hear me at the back?'

'No,' said a voice, 'we can't hear you. But it doesn't matter.'

With normal presentation audiences, don't complicate matters with microphones. But if there is danger of some not hearing, you need amplification.

When I arrived to run an in-company presentation course one wintry day, my voice was reduced to a whisper by laryngitis. My cameraman, with his CCTV gear, gave me a hand microphone, fed my croaks through the TV monitor, and made me audible.

Shy speakers are often unnecessarily scared by mikes. Modern ones are no problem and commonsense rules apply. Clear your throat *before* you approach the mike. Similarly, never make asides or whispered comments near it. The thing is no gentleman, and will record or relay anything it catches. On the other hand, don't back away. You'll fade.

A few confident presenters fancy themselves as stage performers. Unless you have rehearsed it and know what you're doing, don't take a microphone from its stand. Never swing it by the cable, blow into it, bang the head, or drop it—you'll deafen people. Likewise, don't push your face too close; it is not a telephone. It will distort and no audience wants the intimacy of hearing your teeth grinding and crashing.

A microphone can amplify, but not clarify mumbled or swallowed diction. Avoid any sudden peaking of volume. Don't pop your 'P-s' too explosively. If you are normally sibilant (as are some young women), try to reduce the hiss on your 'S' sounds.

If the microphone is on a table or rostrum, avoid finger-strumming, tapping with pen, pencil, or pointer, or jingling coins and keys. They give you percussion as punctuation.

Stand back at a normal distance from a standard microphone and speak up reasonably as if it were not there—not to it, but over and past it.

A chest microphone, hung on a light-weight halter round your neck, can be ignored—unless you wear a rattling necklace. Don't scratch it, nor let it thump on your metal name-badge. (No, it will not pick up your heart beat.)

If you walk about the stage, watch you don't trip on the lead. And when finished, take it off. Don't, as did one of my delegates, walk off heedlessly, dragging the entrails out of the electronics.

It was the microphone that made possible The Beatles, Hitler, Billy Graham, and Elvis Presley. Think what it might do for you!

Mood control. How to psych yourself up for your presentation

A brilliant young projects manager in a book-publishing house faded into vocal scribble towards the end of every sentence in presentations. His directors complained they could not understand what he was trying to tell them.

Sent on a speaking course, he confessed that many things seemed so obvious that they hardly needed saying. Bosses 'ought to know'. He wanted to finish quickly at presentations and sit down—either this, or he went into over-complicated subleties.

He accepted that being concerned only with his own feelings was a self-indulgent attitude, and agreed to try to think from the viewpoint of the audience next time. 'Explain as if they were intelligent twelve-year-olds', I suggested. 'Make yourself urgently concerned to convert them to your ideas.'

A week later, a letter from his training officer said: 'It went home. At a presentation today the chief executive told him that, for the first time, the directors understood exactly what he was putting across.'

Wrong mental attitudes in presenters generally arise from nervousness disguising itself as some other mood—loftiness, impatience, arrogance, boredom.

How can the presenter put himself into the right mood? In sport, they now call it psyching yourself up for a match, a fight, a race, or contest. Every presenter should train himself or herself in a self-discipline which does this trick. Some will need half an hour of solitude; others a pep-talk from a colleague, or a brisk walk round the block. Deep, slow breathing steadies the pulse and calms the mind. Before playing the part of mad Ophelia, actress Claire Bloom used to bang her head against the wall.

Psyching up is not new. The idea that if you act confidently you begin to feel more confident was described by William James, leader of the Pragmatism movement, born in New York of Scottish, Irish, and English forbears. In his monumental *Principles of*

Psychology, James said: 'Action seems to follow feeling, but really action and feeling go together. By regulating the action, which is under the more direct control of the will, we can indirectly regulate the feeling, which is not.

'Thus the sovereign voluntary path to cheerfulness, if our cheerfulness be lost, is to sit cheerfully and to act and speak as if cheerfulness were already there.'

Anyone who doubts William James need only jut his jaw, clench his fists, frown fiercely at himself in a mirror, and he will begin to feel angry for no good reason except that going through the actions makes him feel so.

A presenter can train himself to become the master rather than the minion of his mood. He should do so not just to make himself feel easy but for the better transmission of his message to his audience. Act confidently and you will feel confident.

Motivation and persuasion.
Presentations should ask clients to buy

Hell is waiting for all of us. We are irredeemably condemned to the everlasting torture. Friends will desert us. Illness will hurt us, Bankruptcy maim us. Despondency claim us. . . . *Unless* we invest *now* in 'Wonderful Product X', the salvation balm that soothes damnation away like it had never been!

'Everyone lives by selling something,' said the wise Scottish writer, Robert Louis (*Treasure Island*) Stevenson. But looking at some presentations, you see that the motivation, persuasion, and selling process has been forgotten and omitted. They call for no action from the audience. They put on no pressure.

Part of the planning of every presentation should be to answer the questions 'What do we want them to do?' and 'How are we going to motivate them to do it?' Otherwise it will be a vain exercise.

95

There are dozens of techniques of selling. One is the damnation-salvation gambit (above). You must threaten damnation if you wish to sell salvation. It is notable that Hell has gone out of fashion since the hot gospelling days of John Wesley, two centuries ago, and as a result the churches are empty. Discover a disease and sell a cure, and you're in business.

The most eminent of audiences have needs, wishes, desires, hungers, and requirements. It is the presenter's job to discover what these are and to dwell on them. Every person has a handle. Find it and you have something with which to move him.

Apart from the obvious and everyday benefits that the presenter can offer, there are others more subtle, which appeal to special audiences: to have a happy company; to become famous; to win distinction and a title; social success; financial overkill; sporting eminence; or merely health and fitness.

The standard practice of achieving this is: to make friends with the audience and show we know their problem; to dwell on the glory of the benefits; to picture the hell of missing them; to show how easy it is to have them—through the presenter's proposition.

But because we are too tactful, too respectable, too stiffly professional, and don't wish to appear embarrassingly eager, we tend to avoid actually asking the audience to buy. We are shy of asking plainly 'Can I sell you it? Would you like to buy one?'

Soft selling is a blunt weapon, like trying to stop a burglar with a pillow. Often the salesman fears to ask outright in case he gets 'No' for answer. As the Scottish Marquis of Montrose (eventually hanged) wrote three centuries ago:

> He either fears his fate too much,
> Or his deserts are small,
> That puts it not unto the touch,
> To win or lose it all.

Discover the benefits which appeal most to the client and ask for the business enthusiastically and often.

Multi-media presentation can be fun. But do you truly need it?

Slides brightened, cross-faded, and dimmed. Two girls in grass-skirts talked a commentary alternately from flower-draped mikes either side of the screen, a steel band drowning their voices with bongos. Weird coloured lighting flickered over the audience. Several hundred retailers at tables in the huge ballroom of a Park Lane hotel in London sat bemused. Only when a single stand-up speaker without gimmicks spoke from the stage did they come to life.

Once a frustrated would-be showman gets inspired to use 69 French horns and a herd of trumpeting African elephants to launch his new ice-cream cornet on the waiting world, sanity flies out of the window. The truth is that multi-media fantasias of the wilder kind are an ego trip for somebody, and a fantastic harvest for firms who provide the hardware. But are they worth it? Perhaps *yes* as a preliminary to brainwashing large numbers of people. Dr William Sargent, in his great book *Battle for the Mind*, describes how similar techniques have been used for centuries to increase suggestibility for religious and political conversion.

'No man, however highly civilised,' wrote Aldous Huxley, 'can listen for very long to African drumming, or Indian chanting . . . and retain intact his critical and self-conscious personality. . . . If exposed long enough to the tom-toms and the singing, every one of our philosophers would end by capering and howling with the savages.' Bring on the voodoo drums, then, in a multi-media presentation to indoctrinate masses. When their psyches are hot, whack the imprint of new company gospels on their minds for ever—or at least until next year.

These showpieces need immense powers of organization. Their cost effectiveness should be closely questioned. Perhaps something simpler, done well, would work even better.

Names. Identification and memory aids for presenters and audiences

The well-groomed German bowed slightly, clicked his heels, announced his surname, and crushed my hand bloodless.

The six-foot American clapped me on the back, repeating my name with almost affectionate emphasis half a dozen times in his first four sentences.

It is always flattering and reassuring to be addressed correctly and to know the other man's name. This vocal label, it has been said, is the dearest sound to a person in the whole language.

The English are notoriously bad at recalling names. They're 'Terribly sorry about having forgotten yours, old man.' Or worse, they consistently call you by the wrong name every time you meet.

Getting everybody's name right is vital in the presentation situation. What can be done? UK management author Jacqueline Dineen, in her book *Remembering Made Easy*, suggests four ways, abbreviated below.

1. Listen intently to the name when you first hear it. Ask for it again if you miss it, or have it spelt if difficult.

2. Repeat it frequently to impress it on your memory.

3. Conjure up a mental picture that makes the name unforgettable.

4. Associate first names with characters from history or fiction.

Lists, seating-place placards, and lapel badges—if they are right, complete, large enough, and give the normally used first name, too— can save a deal of confusion.

'I liked the style of that young chap of yours sitting at the end of the table,' said a boss presenter to his opposite number, the chief of the client firm, after a presentation with no name cards.

'Not one of my lot,' said the surprised client. 'Must have been one of yours.'

When people don't know one another at a presentation, everyone should be given a list of the names and jobs of both the presenters and the client audience. If the audience is large, at least the presenters and the client top-brass should be listed on the programme.

On more intimate occasions, prewritten name-cards are useful for positioning people. Don't have them lettered too small and don't waste space on 'Mr' and initials. Give the normally used first name, too.

My way of getting people's name-cards right is to ask them to write their own (having provided them with generous cards and thick markers for the purpose). Nobody ever objects and the spelling is always correct.

Most lapel badges are simply absurd. The background of paper, plastic, or metal is of generous size, with the organization logo huge. The delegate's name beneath is typed an illegible fraction of an inch high. You need a telescope to read it.

The best name-plates for presenters and delegates are issued by Management Centre Europe, in Brussels. Their sticky-backed fabric labels, 9 by 6 centimetres, with heavily typewritten characters twice normal size, adhere readily without damage to clothing. They are easily readable at conversational distance and are colour coded to distinguish speakers, visitors, and staff. They are so trouble-free that you easily forget to take them off. It is startling to be addressed later in a Belgian hotel, a restaurant, or at the airport by complete strangers who mysteriously know your name.

Nerves. How to come to terms with them and use them to your advantage

A certain nervousness is vital. If at the thought of making a speech or presentation, you are smitten with:

> cold feet
> knocking knees
> bowels turned to water
> butterflies in the stomach
> banging heart
> occluded lungs
> constricted throat
> clammy hands
> blurred vision
> roaring in the ears
> twitching of the face
> crawling scalp
> hair on end
> a mouth like a sandpit
> a tongue like a loofah
> a mind gone totally blank

plus a frantic desire to dive headlong from the nearest high window—*be glad!* It simply proves that, properly controlled, you have the emotional potential for enthusing an audience.

All the best speakers feel it. Britain's cucumber-cool ex-Prime Minister, Harold Macmillan, known in his day as 'Unflappable Mac', confessed frankly to extreme nervousness in the first volume of his autobiography, *Winds of Change*. 'I have hardly ever had to make an important speech without feeling violently sick most of the day before . . . even at the end of seven years of Premiership I had the same painful anticipation about Parliamentary Questions as men feel before a race or a battle. . . .

'I was able to conceal if not overcome this nervousness

because I had learnt from childhood that these anxieties were natural, inevitable, and must somehow be endured.'

American President John Kennedy, so youthful and dynamic in style, clasped and unclasped his hands nervously below visible level, hidden by the rostrum.

Britain's resolute first woman Prime Minister, Margaret Thatcher has confessed: 'I feel nervous on every occasion I have to speak.'

Carafes of water, tranquillizers, salt pills for salivation, cigarettes, and pep pills don't help much. If absent, or over-used, they become mantraps.

Extreme over-breathing (hyper-ventilation) before you begin can bring on *petit mal*—a kind of fit from having too much oxygen in the bloodstream. Don't pant, therefore, with anticipation. Rather, to calm yourself before you begin, take several deep breaths, holding each as long as you can before exhaling slowly and gently. This is a trick actors use. Done several times, it will work for you, too.

The best cure of all for terror in business presentation is the risk-free atmosphere training course. Here you will learn how to concentrate on your subject and your audience and to forget your own expendable feelings.

Be warned if your nervousness ever completely disappears. The chances are that you will have become a bore.

Notes. How to prepare and use them for improving your presentation

One Monday evening about eight o'clock, America's beloved ex-President Theodore (Teddy) Roosevelt emerged from the Hotel Gilpatrick, Milwaukee, and climbed into his open car. Off to make a speech, he knew that no good presentation ever happened by accident. He had prepared notes which were literally to be a lifesaver. As he stood waving from the car to the cheering crowd, a lunatic shot him in the chest with a Colt revolver at six-feet range. Like a kick from a horse, it knocked Roosevelt flat, but he scrambled up. He coughed, but no blood came. The bullet had hit the folded 50-page manuscript of his speech, broken a rib, but not entered his lung. Roosevelt drove to the meeting, spoke for 50 minutes (one minute per page), then went to hospital to be treated. The bullet stayed in him the rest of his life.

Although some richly deserve it, not many business presenters get shot. But notes are also useful for deflecting metaphorical bullets. They serve four useful purposes:
1. Make you prepare mentally.
2. Define what is relevant.
3. Exclude the unnecessary.
4. Keep you on course and time.

Presenters who habitually speak without notes are geniuses or misguided. The idea that we should not have notes comes from the old but now disregarded rule of the House of Commons that speeches may not be read. Today, this is broken all the time by front-bench politicians.

Notes and scripts are expected in business. Lord Hill, once chairman of the BBC, said: 'The more serious members of an audience actually prefer the speaker to refresh his memory from notes. It shows that he has taken the trouble to prepare himself for the occasion.'

Your client will hate it if you speak about his business unprepared or while consulting what looks like the back of an envelope. Consciously or not, he takes the appearance of your notes as part of your communication. If you are proposing that he should spend large sums of money, they had better look like an important document.

Never speak from small sheets with tatty, multi-holed top edges that look as if they are ripped from your typist's notebook. Postcards are acceptable for a social occasion. They fit easily into a pocket until wanted. I prefer to fix them together at the corner—Drop only six loose ones, and they can be picked up in 719 wrong arrangements.

103

In business presentations, A4 sheets of paper look best, backed with card to stop trembling. Use one side of the paper and plenty of space. Don't have more than five lines without a break, or your eye may get lost.

For maximum visibility, some presenters have notes typed in capital letters, while others alternate sections in red and black. Special typewriters provide big type for speeches. Handwriting with a fat felt pen can go larger still.

For preparing the wording of notes, there are two main methods. You can compose the complete speech word-for-word, then boil this down to its skeleton. Alternatively, the skilled presenter can compose a skeleton set of notes direct and rely on his instant eloquence to expand it as he goes.

Finally, you can annotate your notes with stage directions. *Don't read them out.* Lord Mancroft, preparing to speak in the House of Lords, found his script marked with mysterious initials: FGSBCSTB, TDB, and WPS. An aide explained. At the beginning, the point was touchy; FGSBCSTB meant 'For God's Sake Be Careful, Stick To Brief'. The middle was dull; TDB was to wake people up: 'Thump Dispatch Box'. The WPS end was to give strength to a poor argument: 'Weak Point—Shout!'

Are your notes good enough for somebody else, in an emergency, to make the presentation for you? If so, they are adequate for you.

Objects and working models can speak for themselves

An actual and conspicuous object, such as a folding ladder or a window frame, helps many a presenter who, without it, would be lost. The audience attention is on the visual, the object itself gives a logical structure to what is said; the presenter is almost a commentator or demonstrator.

If you have a gas stove, a gun, a fishing rod, a printing machine, or a rubber dinghy to present, the device can almost speak for itself. Like bicycle wheels that revolve, motorized pumps that circulate liquid, or windmills that turn, they just need to be large and high enough to be seen, well lit with spotlights, and set against a contrasting background.

Hand-size objects are too small to show as actuality. Like architectural and other models (only large enough for five or six people round a table), they need photographing and blowing up larger as a chart or on a slide. A giant reproduction of a cheque, or a Christmas cracker, enlarges the joy of the presentation.

More seriously, 10 milk bottles, filled with coloured 'blood' and properly capped, demonstrates our normal body's blood content. We can afford to give a pint as a donor. If we lose only four pints

105

by bleeding we pant with the need for more to carry the necessary oxygen around the body.

Even grimmer was the ominous-shaped parcel that Melvyn Belli, the demonstrative American lawyer, brought into court when representing a woman who lost a leg under a San Francisco streetcar. It was wrapped in butcher's paper and tied with rough string. He touched but didn't mention it during the hearing. At the height of his appeal for larger damages, Belli began slowly to unwrap the parcel. Court officials winced. Finally he revealed an artificial leg, 'the marvellous scientific invention my client must wear for the rest of her life'. He won the case.

Unveiling a draped visual is always effective—but vulnerable to failures of electricity, changes of humidity and temperature, and other hazards that can wreck the show at the last minute. Rehearse repeatedly and check again in the final hour. Only the hysterically-laughing giant comedian Tommy Cooper can make a success out of a true fiasco. But you don't want laughter, you want the business.

Obsessive talkers kill customers. What can be done with them?

The managing director harangued the prospective client at length about the virtues of the company from noon onwards. 'My heavens, it's quarter to three,' he said at last. Phoning an Italian restaurant next door, he asked: 'I know you shut at three, but can you serve lunch for a party of twelve if we come along in ten minutes?' They got their spaghetti but lost the business.

People often say the obsessive talker suffers from 'verbal diarrhoea'. The psychologists more respectably label it 'logor-rhoea' (from 'logos', Greek for word, and 'rheo' flow). It is a common symptom of over-anxiety.

106

The malady is not confined to Britain. The public relations manager of a French car manufacturer told me: 'Our chief executive always sums up after a presentation. It regularly takes him three times as long as the original show.'

In Madison Avenue, New York, a customer in a hurry with a million dollars to spend, said that most of the companies he called on were so desperate to show their slides and films about themselves that they forgot what he had come to see them about.

Someone may be brave enough to tell the long-winded man. It's a risk. 'Thank you for your 589-word letter,' I once wrote to a director friend. He never again sent me even a note. But I still believe that the worst reaction to the obsessive talker is a passive one.

Strict rationing of presentation talking time per person, with an appointed time-keeper indicating limits by bell, flashing light, or other device can sometimes instil discipline. One way to set up this disciplined approach is to reverse the presentation role. Ask the team to imagine themselves as the client. Get them relaxed after lunch, then let them say what they truly think about order, timing, emphasis, and approach. A frank group-verdict can't be gainsayed and can have a salutary effect. Somehow the killer-talker must be tamed. As a last resort, give him this page to read, marked for his personal attention. He'll probably think you mean someone else.

Overhead projector. The presenter's friendliest visual aid

You write or draw on a light-table in front of you and the words and pictures shine out on the screen behind and above you. What friendlier aid could a presenter find? You present in normal lighting, but work with a bright image. You don't have to turn your back (as with flipchart or chalk board), and can easily maintain eye contact with your audience. You switch on or off as you please.

The overhead projector (OHP) is thus closely integrated with you and your performance. It is flexible and undemanding, quick and colourful, and relatively inexpensive. It lacks the slickness of slides unless you are a very skilled operator. But it is an ideal working tool where solutions rather than sophistication are the aim of the presentation.

Vision for the audience depends on the positioning of the OHP and of the screen. Some experts like the screen skewed to the audience, with the projector to one side of the stage so that it obscures the view for the fewest possible people. Many tables are too high and many ceilings too low, but in the ideal circumstances, with a screen high enough, the projection is truly over the presenter's head and can be clearly seen by all.

With the beam for the instrument's reflecting mirror ascending at perhaps thirty degrees above the horizontal, the screen then needs to be tipped forward correspondingly. Otherwise the light does not hit the screen at a right angle and the distortion called keystoning results. Intended optical exaggeration and distortion are now so common in photography and TV that, in my view, most audiences don't mind keystoning (wide at the top, narrower at the bottom). If no screen is available, they are even content with a keystoned image projected on to a flat light-coloured wall. The quality of image projected from the acetate transparencies concerns them much more. What is already illegible, misspelt, badly set out, over-crowded, fuzzy, dirty, lacking contrast, too pale or too gloomy, and otherwise chaotic will not improve by being brightly lit and thrown on a screen.

All the elementary rules such as keeping it simple, brief, uncluttered, in colours that show, clean, clear, etc., apply just as much to OHP transparencies as to any other visual.

These foils can be made in four main ways; some of them are do-it-yourself methods which take only minutes.

1. With a spirit or water-based fibre-tipped pen or felt-marker, you can sketch, draw, write, or print freehand direct on the acetate sheet. Some artistic ability is needed to prevent the result

108

looking crude. Squared up graph paper as backing will help keep uprights and horizontals reasonably right. A pencilled rough on a backing helps to space the layout to advantage. A bulldog clip holding acetate and backing stops them moving out of register as you trace the image.

2. Tracing can extend to technical drawings, diagrams, and elementary hand-lettering from originals other than your own roughs. Often this has the advantage that it simplifies what is being traced by quickly taking the bones out of an otherwise over-detailed original.

3. Typing direct can be done on a special carbon-backed white paper, which makes a carbon copy on to its twinned acetate backing sheet. A ball-point pen, hard pencil, or other hard point (but not a fibre-tipped pen) will similarly mark the carbon onto the acetate. To get the best results from typing direct, use a machine with a large typeface, or the result will be too small to read on the screen. Good results can be obtained from a manual typewriter with jumbo capitals half a centimetre high, designed for typing materials for use in infant schools

4. Originals typed, drawn, transfer-lettered, or mounted as collages of assembled bits can be photocopied onto suitable acetates. Brilliant visuals can be composed this way. The worst effect is obtained by photocopying overcrowded typed or print-out material.

Transparencies produced by any of these four methods can be improved by two means. The first is the tasteful introduction of some colour, by pen, marker, or adhesive colour film to brighten an otherwise grey outlook. Even a stripe of red, blue, or green above or below a table of figures gives it character, as does circling vital figures in colour.

Secondly, transparencies can be made more robust by fixing them in standard cardboard frames, which hold them flat and stop them from rolling up or becoming creased.

Some overhead projectors are conveniently fitted with rollers front and back (or either side), carrying a continous sheet of thin acetate film, to be cranked across the light table as required. Visuals can be traced, drawn, or lettered on this in advance in the order to be used and rolled into position as required. Alternatively, the acetate roll can be used for instant visuals, drawn, written, or figured in front of the audience as required. A presenter who has complete command of his subject matter, and who has facility with the special pen for acetate, can provide a fascinating spontaneous show this way.

Handling the transparencies neatly, quickly, and confidently depends on having them stacked (if framed) in the order required, right way round, and right side up. Notches on the frames that fit pegs on the projector make it easier to position them squarely.

Framed transparencies in bulk tend to be weighty to transport. Unframed flimsies are lighter, but clinging. They can be controlled by filing them in a child's thick-leaved scrapbook, one to an opening, the pages correspondingly titled and numbered.

Some presenters switch off between one transparency and the next, some not.

To prevent the audience getting ahead of you, use a blank sheet of paper as a mask, pulling it down to reveal the part of the visual you are talking about. By putting it beneath the transparency, you can see what is coming next and it will not fall off so easily.

You can point to any part of the visual with a finger, pencil, or coin as place-marker on the acetate. To avoid interfering with sight lines, some operators use a pointer on the projected screen image. Purists frown on this practice.

The ultimate OHP techniques are coloured jigsaw pieces to project; assorted overlays to bring in as required from any of the four edges of the cardboard frame, and a motorized polarized disc attachment which gives your prepared picture (such as electrical circuits, roadways, pipes) an illusion of flow. Unless such tricks are essential and can be well rehearsed in advance, it is wise (as with all visuals) to keep to what is simple.

My portable OHP, the size of a briefcase but twice as tall, has only once blown its bulb, despite hundreds of miles of travel and much use. Always carry a spare bulb, handle it with gloves or a duster to avoid finger marks creating a hot-spot on the glass, and know how to install it.

The overhead projector is a kindly tool though not foolproof

110

because, as the man said, fools are so ingenious. My worst experience was controlling a last-hour audience's hilarity when a ladybird, trapped inside, kept legging it across my light-table in silhouette across the screen—enlarged to monster size. I switched off repeatedly to retain the initiative and avoid cooking the insect. We both survived.

P

Pheidippides the Greek. How did he get into this?

Are you concerned about feeling comfortable when you make presentations? Do you look for props and aids to make it easy and help you feel good? Many beginners tell me this is what they seek: enjoyment, content, and well-being. They are affronted when I say that they have their eyes on the wrong objective.

Of the three factors in presentation—speaker, message, audience—the latter two are important, the first expendable. Getting the message right and persuading the audience to 'buy' it is vital.

If the presenter pays in blood, toil, tears and sweat, that is the normal price of victory. It is for this reason that Pheidippides should be (were he not a pagan Greek of 490 BC) the patron saint of presenters. Under an olive tree near Athens, Greece, one blazing June day, an eloquent professor of antiquities from Dublin, Professor John Luce, clad in khaki shorts and a patriarchal beard, told us about the glorious Battle of Marathon in which Pheidippides played such a part. This was a conflict to compare with the Armada or the Battle of Britain. Persia, demanding tribute from the Greeks, had set out to engulf Europe. Some 25 000 Persians attacked 10 000 Athenians at Marathon.

We stood by the tumuli of the mass grave where 192 Athenians had been honourably buried. On the same battlefield had perished 6400 of their foes. A terrific victory, it was aided by Pheidippides who ran 26 miles to Athens (the first 'marathon') for help at the crucial hour. He was intent, as every speaker should be, on getting his message to his audience. Uncaring of his own feelings, he delivered it—and fell dead. An example for all presenters.

Planning the presentation to get it right from the start

Because of the restrictions on time, technicality of subject, special status of the audience, compression of treatment, and the complexity of using several speakers, planning a sound foundation for a presentation is essential. No amount of last minute tinkering will put right mistakes made at the start.

Why are we presenting? To whom are we going to say what? And how shall we say it? Clear-headed thought must be applied first to the overall shape and purpose of the presentation, then individually to each section of the whole.

Creating this plan does not need a full meeting. Two or three sharp minds are enough. Sir Alec Issigonis, creator of the million-selling British Leyland Mini motor car, said: 'I always work with a small team, because I firmly believe that any meeting that has more than three people at it is a waste of time, with more talk than action.'

Shave down the reason for the presentation to a single, sinewy and specific statement, beginning 'To show . . .,' or 'To persuade . . .'. It's a good idea to letter it large and stick it on the wall for all to see. Referring back to this clear objective will settle arguments and doubts as the presentation takes form.

The second question is to define 'Who?' It is horribly easy to gather the wrong audience, who will receive your presentation (and the drinks) rapturously. But, because they are not decision-makers, they will not be able to do anything about it.

The right audience, its attitude of mind, and its state of knowledge must be clearly identified and defined, as well as the effect you aim to have on its thinking and actions. Be totally clear about the reaction and action you seek.

Next comes the 'What?' job of deciding the content that goes into the presentation to achieve these purposes. Gather your ideas roughly in writing. Include the tasty plums you know the audience will enjoy, and cut down on anything that is dull or too detailed. Ration the time severely to less than will be finally allowed; presentations always grow.

The personality, status, and effectiveness of the speakers you intend to bring on have a bearing on 'How?' which is the fourth planning question. The content largely decides the order in which you arrange your sections for lucidity, logic, and achieving the effect you are aiming at. The speakers must be deployed in the best order for 'orchestrating' the message. Never finish with a dull, longwinded section, put over by a weak presenter. At the end of the runway the presentation should take off and *fly*.

Having worked it all out as a plan, bring in the team members. Allot them their tasks. And sell them the idea that they *can* do it.

Presentation. Let's be clear what it is and tries to achieve

Although almost everyone in commerce and industry today talks about, takes part in, watches, and listens to presentations—they are a form of communication peculiar to business.

If you want to learn more about presentation, you won't find much about it in dictionaries or books about speech-making. *The*

115

Concise Oxford Dictionary gives five meanings for the word, including a medical one about the way a baby enters the world. But none about presentation in business.

Yet, every day, scientists make research and development presentations in-company, marketing directors make presentations to the board, chairmen present to government ministries, PR people present to news media, advertising agencies present to clients, sales management present to conferences, and salesmen present to customers. I have even met priests who were attending marketing seminars, presumably to find ways to present their gospel more effectively to the world.

The purpose of a presentation can be defined as: *To put over to small groups of people, in limited time and differing venues, our facts, figures, and ideas by spoken words, aided by visuals, in ways which motivate them to take the action we wish.*

It is an under-statement to say that much may hang on the outcome. 'A bad presenter,' said an advertisement by the 3M Company, 'is a horrifying, even nauseating embarrassment to himself and others.' He can wreck the organization.

The task of effective presentation is tough for several built-in reasons:

1. A presentation consists of a formalized spoken message, which has to be prewritten to control length and accuracy. Writing to length defeats many. Writing for speaking is even harder for most non-professionals. It is dangerously easy to write something that reads smoothly for the eye, but is too stiff to be spoken comfortably.

2. Presentations are generally given by several author-speakers. Their styles need matching and their content must not overlap, nor leave gaps between one section and the next. To achieve this, someone must be overall coordinating editor. He will be more objective and unbiased if he is not one of the presenters. Someone in the position of chairman can prevent the embarrassing situation sometimes seen in TV discussion programmes, when two or even three speak at once, all refusing to give way.

3. Because presenters normally wish to say so much in a limited time, the spoken message must be compressed. The best aid for compression is visuals.

116

4. A presentation has not one purpose but three: first, to show that the presenters understand the problem; second, to put across their solution; and third, to persuade the audience to 'buy' the solution. The first stage is often overplayed, and the final one neglected.

5. The final special tough characteristic of presentation is that the audience has special status. It is like a collection of senior buyers. You are comparable to an advocate speaking before a judge, who can interrupt in a variety of ways if he wishes.

Even if it is done with the kindest intention, a presenter may be thrown by the client who says: 'We know about the problem, thanks. Would you like to skip that part, and move on to your suggestions?'

Time and duration, especially, are at the discretion of the audience. You cannot take the time you want. You have to compress your message into the time allowed. But there are, thank goodness, two saving corollaries which make presentation easier. The first is that in presenting your facts and ideas, there is no need to be exhaustive. As Voltaire, the French satirist, said: 'The secret of being a bore is to tell everything.' The second saving factor is that a successful presentation is seldom the end, but generally the beginning of negotiations. It can be backed up with a document. It will certainly be followed by discussion.

Questions. How to get them coming and when to answer them

As a presenter, you do not have to include everything. You can select and sample. You are successful if you arouse curiosity so that people want to ask for more.

So: question time! How do you handle it? The first decision is whether to take questions as they arise, or ask the audience to keep them for a subsequent question session.

A lone presenter, knowing the subject thoroughly and presenting to a small group, can take questions as they come. If mentally quick on his feet, he can use the participation to keep the presentation lively, while still allowing his inner 'automatic pilot' to pull the presentation back on course if it drifts.

More complicated multi-speaker presentations, building up an intricate structure of fact and persuasion, work best when questions are corralled into special between-time sessions, or confined to one major question time at the end. In this situation, it helps to have a senior chairman who will call on his speakers as required, sometimes judging whether a question, for reasons of policy, is admissible or not. He can also control which question comes next, give fair shares to all, and help maintain good tone in the meeting.

119

What can you do when the meeting is formally thrown open to questions *and none comes?* There are five good ways to get round this:

1. Inform the audience clearly at the opening of the presentation that questions will be welcome at a certain time. 'Please make a mental note of any that arise in your mind as we go on. They will be welcome at question time.' Audiences usually play by the rules if these are plainly defined.

2. The chairman can break the silence by asking a prepared question himself, 'Taking advantage of my position before everybody else rushes in.' This should get questions rolling.

3. An official question-starter can be recruited.

4. If desperate, the chairman or speaker can call upon a known person by name to volunteer a question. Choose someone reliable, or he may embarrassingly refuse or even walk out.

5. A final desperate expedient is for the speaker to pose a question to himself: 'Many people ask . . .' or 'It arose the other day . . .' or some such excuse. Anything which breaks the inhibiting spell of silence will start the genuine questions coming.

Handled aright, question time should be the warmest and most rewarding part of presentation. The verbal communication traffic is now two-way. The livelier it becomes, probably the more successful the presentation has been.

Question time. Twelve moves for answering effectively and getting good mileage

Questions, in my view, are not launched to be shot down. They can be used constructively to further your case. One famous BBC executive, whom I invited to address a club, would not make a speech, but offered to answer questions. We got some good ones ready for him, and he provided us with a sparkling evening.

Once the positive attitude is accepted, we can study the best ways of getting good mileage from question-answering. Here is a survey of techniques under four headings:

Receiving questions. Smile and look interested, not nervous, lofty, or aggressive. Listen well.

I once saw ex-Labour Prime Minister Jim Callaghan taking a question from a little old lady in the middle of a large audience. He invited her to the front so that he could hear her better. He listened encouragingly. He nodded and smiled. When it came to the point, he had to refer her to the local housing officer, but his courteous manner had won the audience's high regard.

With large audiences who don't all hear the question, or with an untidy question, it pays to repeat the crux of it before answering. Don't give the crux of a different question which you feel better able to answer. The twist is always noticed.

At the same time, refuse to accept a question that is abusive or based on a false premiss. 'Have you stopped defrauding your customers yet?' contains an insult to which no honest person can submit.

It is this kind of falsely based question which leads presenters to say: 'Let's get the question right for a start.' But say it with a smile.

Your manner in answering should be tactful and kind. Shy people put their feelings at risk by asking a question. They need reassuring that it is sensible.

If there are several queries in one, separate them, perhaps using a scribbled note to remember the parts.

A question which is irrelevant for others can be answered quickly, or the questioner given a time later to discuss it privately.

Be complimentary if you can. 'That's a penetrating question.' Laughing: 'You *are* a friend to ask that one!' Or 'They're bowling them fast today, Mr Chairman.' Audiences warm up as you appreciate them.

Try to address the answer to all, not just the questioner. This is good meetings procedure. The question having been accepted by the chairman and/or speaker becomes the 'possession' of the meeting. Thus the answer should logically be addressed to everyone present, so that nobody is ignored and all are engaged. The speaker who forgets he is talking to a group, and not to single people, can easily lose control by allowing a dialogue to develop with just one person. If he unwisely asks 'Does that answer your question?' he is inviting dialogue and possibly disagreement.

The material used in answering should stick to the ABC of the subject. Keep answers simple.

Quote a case history, an example, or a little story if you can. Nothing illustrates a point better than a fitting and vivid anecdote.

If your answer wanders towards a ragged end, tidy it by recapitulating the question and giving the pith of the answer as final summary.

The end result of question time should be a closer bond of communication, respect, and even affection between the audience and the presenter. To achieve this, avoid argument and don't dispute small unimportant facts. Let the opinionated person have his say and make a friend of him. Give way graciously, or at least win with goodwill.

At the Production Engineering Research Association at Melton Mowbray, I was warned about one of the 400 audience. The organizers pointed him out. 'He's had every presenter so far, and he'll have you,' they said. Sure enough, at question time, he grabbed the roving microphone. Everyone expected a thoroughly nasty question, but I got in first.

'Hello,' I said laughingly, 'they warned me about you. Three rows back, right side, against the gangway. That is you, isn't it? Ladies and gentlemen, they told me that this gentleman is a terror. He looks all right to me. Let's give him a round of applause.' I started to clap and everyone laughed and joined in. The aggressive questioner was tamed before he started.

What many presenters fear most is being shot down by a question they cannot answer. No need to worry. When you don't know, don't waffle but do keep cheerful. Appreciate the question that threatens to stump you. Be grateful for the opportunity to learn more. Promise that you will find out and will let the questioner and any other interested parties know later.

122

Always be courteous and stay friends with your audience. Let no one ever say 'I know him, he made a fool of me at question time once in front of half the industry.' That will be held against you for ever.

The final impression you must leave with your audience is that you are a pleasant person, who knows his stuff thoroughly and enjoys presenting his case, company, profession, industry, or country. That is question time success.

R

Reading aloud well in presentation—instead of sounding pathetic

Fifty young men, all under forty, standing around the dining table in an Essex country house, hushed their chatter. One of them spoke the Round Table 'Promise'. Unlike so many who read out aims and objectives, he made it sound impressive and inspiring. Not dismal, pathetic, and ashamed. I felt proud to be there.

Sooner or later, every business presenter has to read out something to a group. Most can't do well what should be an easy duty. You'd think some were word-blind. Obviously, they haven't read aloud since they left the third grade at school. You can hear the painful accent of short trousers or blue gym slips. They mumble like an elderly hen scurrying to get out of the rain. The year's results may be fantastically good. But the reading damps enthusiasm.

How can you avoid the pathetic cross between a gabble and a drone and become reasonably competent at reading out loud?

1. Make sure the passage is physically easily readable. Don't fumble to find the page, peer at small type, miss out bits. Even if you're quoting an official report, have your part typed out large, with plenty of margin, at least double-spaced. Give yourself a chance to read well.

2. Rehearse it full voice in private. If circumstances make this impossible, mutter it through silently with moving lips. This will give you fair warning of mistakes, double meanings, tongue-twisting traps, and pronunciation difficulties. Mark up the script, if you can, to point the phrase, emphasize words, and maintain the pitch to the sentence-end.

3. As you rehearse, try to preread, keeping your eye running a line or two ahead of your voice. Never read one word at a time.

4. Hold the paper high, so that your eye can glance from the words to the audience without you having to nod like a lovesick duck.

You *know* how your reading should sound: easy, clear, unembarrassed, and with variations of tone, pitch, pace, and volume. Speed is the enemy. Take it easy. Be natural and interesting. There is plenty of scope. The English alphabet contains a code of more than 2000 rules of pronunciation.

Raise your standard by listening to a good reader on radio or television. Put in some non-business practice:

1. Read sometimes to invalids or the blind.

2. When he was first made a marketing director, my friend Peter Finch read the lessons in church—for his own and others' good.

3. Read titbits from letters or the newspaper at breakfast.

4. Read to your children at bedtime. Your personal rendering of *Winnie the Pooh*, Enid Blyton, *Alice in Wonderland, Treasure Island,* Tolkien, or *Watership Down* will beat television for them.

5. Finally, why not, as I do, read poetry to one's spouse in bed? Your reading will improve and your partner's insomnia will vanish.

Refreshments are the most welcome of all presentations

Delegates to College of Marketing presentation courses at Moor

Hall, Cookham, near Maidenhead, meet on arrival the first morning over coffee and biscuits. A cup of tea or coffee says 'Hello and welcome' more sincerely than the warmest of words.

The answer to 'How soon with refreshments?' at a presentation is, generally, that it is *never* too soon.

The biggest of business brains can be relied upon to remember the quality of food and drink provided at any presentation. Why then scrimp or save trouble on this important hospitality? Machine-made liquid served in plastic cups may be a popular economy for staff, but is an insult to clients. The single dusty plate of dry biscuits (from which a quick junior has nicked the only sugared or chocolate one) is likewise a disgrace.

Treat your guests as hospitably as you would in your own home. Choice should be wide: coffee or tea, coke or soft-drinks, if preferred; or alcohol for those who need it. One hotel at London Heathrow Airport offers soft drinks with the normal iced water on meetings tables, plus barley sugar sweets. Everyone enjoys them.

Moving the group into a lounge or lobby for refreshments is a good plan. Presentation audiences will not complain if offered two refreshment breaks in a morning or afternoon. Few of them ever sit in their own offices for more than half an hour without moving from their chairs. Each respite gives a valuable chance for leg-stretching, discussion, and mingling.

At a morning break, why not offer menus from which they can choose and order lunch? Not everyone wants your idea of a set meal.

If it will not bring the whole canteen and staff restaurant staff out on strike, it may be desirable to have some of your comeliest of secretaries acting as hostesses with refreshments.

FHB (family hold back) should apply: clients first, presenters next, and support staff afterwards.

In your enthusiasm to tell your presentation story, never forget the heart makes many decisions and is nearer to the stomach than to the head. Don't be late for lunch.

Rehearsals—how many, when, and how conducted?

Not even the top boss himself should be allowed to make a presentation unrehearsed. Stress causes unprecedented and nightmare errors. I have witnessed the agony of a chief executive, after a good lunch, who could not conclude his 'brief introduction' but talked on and on. The director of another company mistakenly praised by name, before the presentation, the rival national product instead of his own.

Others who wish to avoid rehearsal often say it will make them wooden. But this is true only if they rehearse wrongly and without a knowledgeable expert to coach them.

Stage-by-stage rehearsals provide intermediate deadlines, which ensure that production of a presentation is proceeding on schedule. They preclude the panic, the crises, and the chaos that arise from things being left to the last minute, which causes everyone to have to work half the night.

For a presentation conference of a score of scientific papers last October, we staged the first rehearsal in April and held three more before the final show, which went successfully without a hitch to three days of multi-national audiences.

Let everyone know in advance how many check-ups, read-throughs, visuals conferences, monitoring meetings, rehearsals, and final polishings you plan to have. Make it clear when and where they will take place and what stage of development will be expected at each. Issue everyone with a programme of this schedule and make it a command performance each time. You will need a progress chaser to see that people do the work, remember the meetings, and turn up on time.

Rehearsal No. 1 will look at the presenters' notes to check what they intend to say. Gaps, overlapping, and divergence of facts and opinions have to be pruned out.

Rehearsal No. 2 should run through the rough scripts, which should be ready by now. At this stage they should be shortish

Well spaced rehearsals always pay. They reassure the presenter, reinsure the presentation, and finally reward the audience.

rather than long and the visual ideas can be represented verbally, by flipchart or blackboard scribbles, or by quick overhead projector transparencies.

Following this, the person responsible for producing the visuals can get going on what each presenter requires.

If there is to be a documentary back-up, the presenters can produce the précis of their part at this stage for editing into the whole. Each can also work on achieving speakability with his script, instead of letting it congeal into an inhuman stiffness.

Rehearsal No. 3 should include everything and everybody. Sometimes it can be done on a one-at-a-time basis, with the audience fluctuating from a few to a handful, as each presenter brings colleagues or not. The order in which presenters will appear is not necessarily followed. But the final show is all more or less on parade, a bit at a time, in rough form.

This is the moment for a rigorous time-checking. Surgery now saves agony later. Visuals must be monitored for suitability and for errors, and presenters coached in their handling of them. Be complimentary but ruthless. We can't rehearse promises. The actual stuff has got to be here and must be worked on firmly.

This penultimate rehearsal is the now-or-never one. There is not going to be another chance to shape the overall presentation, get visuals and speakers into the most effective order, ensure that time-keeping is *right* (not a matter of hopes and promises), and finish confident that the whole is going to work well.

Rehearsal No. 4 should be held in the actual presentation room or the nearest approach to it that is possible. Everything and everybody must be arranged to run through a serious and non-stop rehearsal, as if it were the actual day. This is no time for criticism—only encouragement. No time for change—only the removal of unforseen snags. Because it is a dress rehearsal, everybody should be dressed as on the day and a fairly numerous and cooperative audience should be present throughout. Nothing should hold up or interrupt the start-to-finish flow, and all extra work must be relegated until after the rehearsal.

Personal rehearsal. Before, between, and after any of the official rehearsals, any single person can work alone or be specially coached by someone. Reading something silently to yourself can hardly be called rehearsing. But talking out loud, standing in front of an imaginary audience, or to a tape recorder or video camera should definitely help (you can listen and look afterwards as critically and coolly as you please).

Most beginners, however, need an expert on presentation to listen to them, or they may well groove themselves into an immovably bad version of what they can do. This is the kind of 'wrong rehearsal' that makes presenters stale and parrot-like.

A small panel of producers is best for rehearsing highly technical presentations: one to look at the personal presentation and speaking; one on technicality and company policy; and one on visuals and practicalities.

Of course, some first-class presentations are produced almost overnight by experienced experts, with only rudimentary rehearsal. These are the exceptions. Most presentations lack preparation, but rehearsals usually accelerate the job rather than retard it, because they act as progress checks.

Rehearsal is essential. Nothing has changed in 600 years since Geoffrey Chaucer's day: 'Who-so shal telle a tale. . . . He must reherce, as ny as ever he can, Everich a word.'

S

Shape of a presentation. Arranging the parts to get maximum results

Some presentations are like the legendary Bumblebee: aerodynamically so unsound that they fly only because nobody realizes they can't.

A new business presentation in an ageing advertising agency started with the chairman making a threadbare pun on his company name. Evidently he'd done it as his opening quip a thousand times. Silent groans! But then two youngsters came on stage, with the exciting story of a new fast-growing business. This was encouraging. Alas, the final anchor piece was a 20-year old tale of a product the agency had handled for a generation. Two bowed grandfathers presented it. 'Grow old along with me!' as Robert Browning wrote. Nobody wanted to.

A clean clear shape to a presentation backed by a visual of the contents list, which can be brought back as a reminder when appropriate, helps the audience to follow what is going on.

Any spoken message, presentation, or speech needs four parts to shape it in a way that will work. They can be variously described.

First, the opening lines are a means of 'switching on' the audience. No use transmitting until the receivers are working.

After that, the rustic preacher's simple pattern for his highly successful sermons cannot be bettered:
1. 'First I tell 'em what I'm *going to tell* 'em.
2. 'Next, I tell 'em what I'm *telling* 'em.
3. 'Then I tell 'em what I've *told* 'em.'

The concept of verbal shape, of engineering a message's structure in ways that will make it work best, is not easy (without literary interest or training) to grasp. Yet all verbal communications that continue in a line through time make use of such structuring —songs, plays, stories, speeches, novels, music, verse, and presentations. Some forms are highly structured. The classical sonnet is made entirely of 10-syllable lines (called iambic pentameters). It is a poem of 14 such lines, divided into eight and six (octave and sestet), or three sets of four lines (quatrains) plus a final couplet, with rhymes in a fixed pattern.

Nobody is suggesting that a presentation should be crystallized and cut into such verbal jewellery as this. But a clear shape puts the facts and ideas in a neat box, instead of thrown together like dirty washing in a bedsheet.

The overall shape of a presentation and the shape of its internal parts can well be based on refinements of that employed by the preacher above. We can still divide it into four stages.
1. Making friendly contact with the audience. Fools rush in where professionals take their time. Appearing too slick and smart makes clients feel uncomfortable.

David Ogilvy, founder of Ogilvy, Benson, and Mather, said that in America he was nervous of his English accent. He therefore opened with axioms nobody could question, until they got used to the way he spoke.

The audience has to tune in. It also has to be made to warm to us, and perhaps get a glimpse of our authority to speak. Here is a wonderful example of a warmer. The toastmaster at the banquet bangs the table, roaring out: 'My Lords, Ladies and Gentlemen, pray silence for Lord Boothby of Buchan and Rattray Head, Knight Commander of the Order of the British Empire, Doctor of Laws, Lord Boothby!'

Boothby gets up, grins around, and says in gravelly bass: 'It's only me!'

Modesty isn't amusing unless, like Bob Boothby, you have a lot to be modest about. Generally it is better to talk about the client rather than yourself.

2. The second stage is to define *why* you are presenting and *how* you will handle your subject matter. This does not need to be long, but it should be said lucidly, clearly, and unmistakably.

The first of these—*why*—is often taken for granted. Presenters assume that audiences know or will guess why they are talking about something. But it clears the mind and sharpens the reactions of all concerned if a purpose is actively set out, not just passively implied.

Instead of the mute understanding that a deal would be pleasant, an audience is more likely to be moved when you say 'We would be proud to have your business. And we would like to tell you how this would benefit you'.

The salesman of a certain British radio manufacturer naturally knew they were expected to compete against rival companies. But they became inspired when the new American managing director said extravagantly at the sales conference: 'We have no wish to hamper or inconvenience our competitors in the market. We merely intend to knock them down and kick their teeth in!'

The second part of this programming stage is to tell the audience clearly in advance the 'chapter headings' of what you are going to say. The obvious objection to this is 'Aren't you giving the game away if you tell people in advance what they will hear?' Not so. Nothing is pre-empted by the right kind of heading or description. The final section of a fat book on selling by an American computer salesman named Robert Burns, for instance, was headed 'Selling Secret No. 6—A Powerful New Closing Technique'. Enticing, yes. But a give away? Not at all!

The programme of a presentation should be a short list of intriguing promises. They should be arranged in increasing order of interest, impact, and importance. Each should be explicit without being long-winded, short without being laconic or meaningless. Studying tabloid newspaper headline-writing will show you how to do this.

It is desirable with three or four sections, and imperative with five or six, to have the headings displayed visually to the audience. A flipchart list that can be ticked as you progresss is one useful way. A continuity slide is another, with the current section coming up coded in a different colour (yellow, say, instead of white reversed on black).

3. Stage three is the largest: it is the actual body of the presentation. Strangely, it is necessary to say the obvious about this: that it should follow the programme promised in stage two.

A proportion of presenters, for some illogical reason, announce that they will deal, for instance, with A, B, and C—and then start with C! Varying from a pre-stated ABC to an order of CBA, BCA, or other of the possible six variations can only confuse the audience.

Try to give each section of the presentation a reasonably equal length, weight, and number of visuals, otherwise one will outweigh others. Ensure that the audience realizes when you have finished one part and are starting the next. See that each section has a clear beginning and is summed up neatly before passing to the next.

Audiences like to know where they are, how far they have progressed, and how much more is to come. The feeling of progression keeps them hopeful. Like the sailors with Christopher Columbus before he reached America, they hate to be sailing on endlessly without reaching anywhere. Sight of a landfall, the end of the voyage, excites them like sailors reaching port.

4. Stage four is where the presenter wraps up his parcel of facts and ideas in one take-away package. It should reiterate the original *why*, and it should summarise the body of the presentation—the *how*. The audience should be able to accept it as the clear crystallization of the whole message. It should be encouraging, optimistic, and able to motivate them.

This kind of structuring not only applies in miniature to, say, 10 or 20 minutes of verbal communication. It also can be magnified to cover a day, two days, or three. The same laws of (1) contact, (2) prediction, (3) performance, and (4) summary still apply.

The material that a presentation puts across varies according to the occasion. Often it falls into three parts, each with its opportunities and hazards.

The first is 'We understand your problems'. This is a great

opportunity for tuning in. But don't push your luck too far. Go into too much detail and you may become boring, or prove you don't know the problem.

The second part is 'Our suggested solution'. Stand back from the work you have prepared before you begin to present it. Get it into perspective. Otherwise, all your struggles, labour, and sweat will get into the script. That's what you're employed for and the client does not wish to know about it. All he wants revealed to him, with a 'Hey, presto!' and a touch of glamour and glory, is the bright result of your toil. Don't show the muddy digging: display the brilliant diamond.

The third part of the content is what salesmen call 'the close'—to ask for your ideas to be adopted. English good manners sometimes inhibit otherwise good presenters at this point. We should never neglect to ask.

My friend Joe Rubin, then marketing director at Marela Pickles, used to cry agonizingly to salesmen: 'Never leave out the gimme-the-order bit!' He was right.

Showmanship is a part of presentation success

In pictures and words, the Robin is a much-publicized bird. But what is it? Little more than a drab sparrow in a red Christmas waistcoat. Showmanship wins! Omitting showmanship from your presentation puts it in danger of becoming mundane.

We are not talking about the logicality and content of the presentation, nor about how appropriate or numerous are the visual aids. We are concerned with the colour, the panache, the glitter, the surprises, and the excitement that gift-wraps the concept and gives it glamour.

Showmanship is a differentiating stripe of colour on each of your statistics transparencies. It is the company logo as a 'signature' in the bottom right corner of each photoslide of a product. It is different coloured tint backgrounds to your black-and-white diagrams and sketches to give them variety instead of leaving them bleak.

Showmanship may be a little suitable canned music as people assemble; an extra spotlight on sideshows of products; or, as background, a simplified map of the world to show the capital cities where you have customers, factories, and offices. It can be a welcome on mock-ups of newspaper posters; it can be a display of flowers or flags. At lunch it can be something to flatter the visitors; their names on bottles of wine. Another way is something to take home for the ladies or for the children—in Southern United States' dialect they have the word 'lagniappe', a small gift for a customer. Good idea!

Where is this brightening most necessary? Run through the presentation and put the finger on spots that are long-winded, monotonous, and dull. What can be done about them?

Can a pretty woman, instead of a lugubrious man, take a 10-minute section for some good reason? Can someone appear in costume? Can dull headings be replaced by flamboyant banners? Can notions that you wish to destroy be represented by labelled balloons burst with a pin or lighted cigarette?

Can you employ an instant questionnaire for the audience to tick or cross? Can the dull passage be cut entirely, or covered by a document to hand out at the end? Can the document be colourful, instead of being merely a bundle of white paper?

Somehow, the fabric of the presentation has to be made brighter, the excitement raised, the goods put on an attractive exhibition stand, and the showbiz element injected. It must not be silly, nor feeble, nor overdone. The level at which you pitch it depends on the product, the occasion, and the seniority of the audience.

Nobody can define how to put showmanship into presentations in general. It is a creative job, depending on inspiration and flair. The actor Barry Humphries, when appearing as the outrageous Australian matron, 'Edna Everage', ends the show by throwing gladioli to the audience. They wave them in unison and often playfully beat one another over the head with them.

How did a great newspaper publishing house present the relaunch of a children's comic to waiting journalists and photographers? A huge all-in wrestler, stripped to fight, astride the bonnet of a tiny car, burst through a screen, waving copies in the air and bellowing its name like a challenge. Perhaps this is not something for your next presentation, but an excellent example of memorable showmanship.

Slides are tops for slick presentations

Slides are the favourite visual aids for glossy and important presentations. They are brighter and slicker than other visuals. Prepared professionally and controlled automatically, they give a sense of confident certainty.

Unless back projected, slides require a darkened room, which is better obtained by dimming with a rheostat than suddenly switching the lights out.

The slide projector must be further from the screen than with an overhead projector. If there is no projection room, this generally means finding a place for it on a stand centrally among the audience, or possibly in a middle gangway.

Experts recommend that the screen is best arranged at a minimum of 2.5 screen widths from the front of the audience and a maximum of 6.0 screen widths from the back row.

The audience themselves are best arranged in a 60-degree sector fanning out from the screen. Check what it is like sitting in the seats closest, furthest, and at the sides of the room to ensure the people there can see.

Slides have the great advantage that they can show photographs brilliantly and in colour. There are half-a-dozen sensible precautions to take when making them.

1. Keep the frame well-filled. Don't have so much space wasted

around the photographed object that it appears like a pawn in a desert.

2. Include some kind of scale in photographs. Is that object three inches or a foot in diameter? An inch or centimetre scale, a matchbox or a hand photographed with the object immediately establishes the size.

3. Make sure the slide is bright and photographed against a clean background. Look at a mail order catalogue for examples of brilliant photography.

4. Keep it uncluttered. Technical slides often show too much. They should simplify the concept and leave room for the presenter to explain things—not replace him with something that needs prolonged detailed study by the audience.

5. Don't over-crowd. Informational graphs, figures, and tabulated facts are often too closely packed. No slide should ever look like a page from a railway guide. It is a signpost, not a reference book.

6. Ensure readability. Never use lettering that is too small for the audience to read. Split the material into several slides and use larger letters.

Given good slides, you still need expertise to make the best use of them. To keep your presentation bright, sometimes talk about a slide before it goes up, flashing others through quickly without dwelling on them, and then perhaps making much of a special one.

Avoid the pedestrian rhythm of repeating 'and my next slide shows'. It sends audiences to sleep. Unless held for a reason, any slide should be removed once it has made its point. If the next is not to be introduced yet, a blank tinted slide can be used as a spacer.

Any unexpected slide which surprises you shows bad organization. Don't apologize. Say something bright to cover the slip.

Before you begin your slide presentation, take precautions for avoiding foul-ups.

Check and recheck slides against script and realize that their fixed position removes much of your verbal flexibility.

Avoid making last minute cuts or changes of order. It leads to mistakes.

If a slide is due to come up again, use a duplicate for this. Use more than one carousel rather than risking reloading.

Obviously, you must have a power lead and controls lead of sufficient length. Make sure you practise with the controls.

Know how to position the projector right for the screen. Be totally familiar how the forward-back-focus hand-control works. Know how to switch the projector on and off. Know how to place the carousel in position, how to get the last slide out of the projector (it is often left behind), and how to remove and change carousels.

When you get into back projection, cross-fading with two projectors, voice-integrated slides, and other sophistications, you need the guidance and assistance of an expert projectionist.

Slides tend to take longer to prepare than other visuals, they are much less correctable, and can be expensive. One electronics company spent a large sum on slides for scientific presentations at a two-day conference, but many of them were corrected, omitted, or replaced with others—£500 wasted. Next time the boffins worked up the visuals as overhead projector transparencies and saved money by having only the final versions made into slides.

However brilliant the slides, the presenter should be master, not a pale commentator on a series of projections. He should come through as a speaker whose words are made even more vivid by his visual aid.

Smiling helps to switch on your audience—even if you are in agony

To any audience but a solemn convention of morticians and undertakers, a smile is the easiest and quickest, first and most acceptable communication a speaker or presenter can make. 'Although few simple sign-stimulus patterns operate as releasers in man, there is one of great importance—the smile,' says Julian Huxley. Even young babies will respond, he adds, 'to a crude drawing of a human face, provided that the sides of the mouth turn up. The smiling-face pattern acts as a releaser to a built-in response.'

Smiling helps *you* to switch on your audience. 'A smile is the shortest distance between human beings,' says Austrian Airlines.

A few special smiles are suspect. Remember *Alice in Wonderland*'s crocodile: 'How cheerfully he seems to grin, how neatly spreads his claws, and welcomes little fishes in with gently smiling jaws.'

But otherwise, if your face is stiff with nervousness, and your knees smite one against the other, nevertheless *smile*! Winch up the corners of the mouth. Give the front teeth some fresh air (it's good for them). You will then possibly appear as if transfixed in a horrifying rictus. But you have not finished. *Now* half-close the eyes and your grimace will convert to the semblance of the intended smile. Keep it up! The audience will smile back; the self-perpetuating goodwill feedback-circuit will be established between you.

Too artificial? Think of those smiling, prancing showgirls who always cheer everyone up so much. Some of them *must* have corns, stiff backs, tummy aches, or hangovers from the night before. But who would ever know? They smile and we assume they are happy. So we are happy, too. You can pull off the same emotional *confidence* trick in your presentation.

Smoking when presenting. Avoid it, and beware wily pipe-smokers

As an effective presenter, you have more than enough to do while paying attention to delivery, message, timing, visuals, and audience. Why complicate it all by smoking?

Cigarette extraction, lighting, sucking, fiddling, smoke-puffing, ashtray location, fag-tapping, and finally mangling out—these only needlessly hinder your job of speaking. Moreover, this air-polluting medieval perversion shows disrespect for an audience, much as would gum-chewing or licking lollipops. Executives assembled to receive a presentation do not come to watch your self-indulgences.

Train yourself, therefore, to make your presentation without the self-comfort of something to suck. (And that goes for mints too.) Forget your strange hungers and concentrate instead on your message and audience.

Remember also that there is little more insulting to a chairman than to have half-dead cigarettes crushed into the ashtray in front of him, especially if he is not using it himself.

Cigar-smoking, especially in small ill-ventilated rooms and presentation theatres, though regarded by its perpetrators as the index of opulence and hedonism, is crudely anti-social when non-smokers are present.

Pipe-smoking is even worse when presenting. Some unthinking businessmen tend to feel at ease with a pipe-smoker because he so patiently puffs and listens. Obviously, he is unlikely to act aggressively while tending his private bonfire. Is he not, in fact, peacefully sucking, like a babe at the breast or bottle? He is not likely to start a fight. But he plots.

Don't tell me it's manly. What is so virile about biting on a wooden dummy in public? If they be indulged at all, such infantile habits should be kept for private moments.

I have seen mesmerized men in important business meetings incredibly wait and watch while the pipeman tamps, knocks, scrapes, loads, and relights his totem before deigning to speak. Pipe-smoking is a sanctioned (if not sanctified) style of casting male spells and releasing farmyard smells indoors.

Maybe, to establish business detente, pipe-smoking could occasionally help. Red Indians passed round the Pipe of Peace, and perhaps the harmful internecine struggles of warring boardrooms could be cooled likewise.

Smoke-screens are not put up at presentations without reason. What is being hidden? Pipemanship is a tricky game. Watch out!

143

Spoken word. Its resurgence makes presentation increasingly important

Walk down the Strand from Fleet Street, in London, and you will find, opposite the Law Courts, a picturesque wooden-framed building that survived the 1666 Great Fire of London. This is the Wig and Pen Club (*wig* for lawyers and *pen* for journalists) of which I am a Life Member. Inside, on the wall, is a framed copy of the first advertisement printed by William Caxton.

After he started England's first press in Westminster, Caxton and his successors had a 500-year run with mass communication all to themselves. Now the monopoly is over.

Within a centenarian's lifetime, a Scotsman (Alexander Graham Bell), an American (Thomas Alva Edison), and an Irish-Italian (Guglielmo Marconi), with various Danes and Germans, have given the spoken word greater power than ever before in the history of the world.

1. You can pick up your phone and talk in minutes to a client literally at the other end of the world.

2. Outdoors, a man may address an audience so vast that he needs field-glasses to see the extent of it.

3. Multi-millions of illiterates who cannot read will now never need to learn.

4. Theoretically it is technically possible for one saviour or one megalomaniac to address the whole human race at one moment in time—allowing only for the brief delay in transmitting half-way round the world.

5. All these voices can be preserved for ever.

Although we take them for granted, these concepts are staggering. Others are following. Already it is possible to speed up recorded speech to three times normal with a variable speech control system that avoids distortion, maintains normal pitch, and keeps it understandable. Average speaking (150–175 words per minute) is half the speed of silent reading (250–350 w.p.m.). Speech speeded to 400 w.p.m., therefore, can be reviewed much faster than either.

144

After 2000 generations, the voice has at last caught up with print. We are only at the beginning of a vast revolution, the resurgence of the spoken word. A sound or video summary of a presentation to give to everyone as they leave? Nothing to it! You can do it tomorrow.

Stammering, stuttering, and speech impediments need not stop you

'Hidden by the tongue-tied contortions of the stammerer there almost always lurks a worthwhile and efficient personality. The stammerer should think of himself as disguised by a mask, instead of accepting the stammer as part of himself.' I am not a speech therapist. These are the words of my late friend Dr MacDonald Ladell, a medical psychologist who treated many speech disabilities successfully. We often discussed the subject when he wrote his book about it.

Certain facts about stammering are obvious. For a start, no stammerer does it all the time. Therefore the cause is not in the physical speaking machinery, but is psychological and concerns the emotions. It follows that stammering is not an inherited physical disability; it is often acquired by unconscious imitation, as anyone will agree who has ever found himself 'catching' somebody else's stammer.

The psychological cause is generally recognized as too much heavy discipline from a parent figure at an early stage of childhood. King George VI stammered, and it is notable that his disciplinarian father, bearded George V, once said: 'I was afraid of my father, and I don't see why my sons should not be afraid of me.'

A stammer is usually reckoned to have at its root the conflict between self-assertion and fear of speaking up. But 'stammerers provide a field day for the amateur psychologist,' says Margaret Drabble, who was a stammerer herself before she broadcast about it.

Like any neurosis, stammering is a mixture of advantages and disavantages—though this, and all I have written above, may be strongly disputed by some people. Stammering makes the audience wait. It forces them to listen. It often give exquisite timing to a final word.

In the adult it can become a kind of unconscious aggression against an audience. While the stammerer apparently suffers, there is no doubt that his listeners feel uncomfortable, too. It must be added that experts say none of this happens as a result of a conscious intent.

Stammering and stuttering are symptoms of anxiety. About one in every hundred people suffers from them. They arise most frequently in my experience when (rightly or wrongly) the stammerer feels himself threatened by an occasion, or likely to be heavily criticized or blamed. This fear can, like many others, be irrational.

When they are told this in advance, I find, stammerers usually have little or no trouble speaking without impediment on a presentation course.

Few women stammer. The men who do are generally strong personalities, efficient, ambitious, highly self-disciplined, and sometimes aggressively touchy. The famous author Somerset Maugham (a stammerer who halted conversation) had the reputation of being difficult. 'Many of his friends,' said writer Alec Waugh, 'complained that they could never feel at ease with him.'

All sorts of cures are offered to stammerers. Clubs, courses, singing, hypnosis, psychoanalysis, rhythm speech, metronomes, white noise, electronic devices, and many more. But of course they cannot be cured against their will. One top London executive told me with proud defiance: 'My directors are sending me to a specialist. Poor man! I don't mind listening to him talk. But he won't make any difference to *me*.'

If you really want to make effective presentations, don't let an impediment stop you. Some very talented speakers were once,

146

and sometimes still are, stammerers. Patrick Campbell was a TV star whose stammer gave hope to hundreds like him. Demosthenes, the greatest Athenian orator of all time, was a stammerer. He cured himself by putting seashore pebbles in his mouth, and declaiming to the Greek god Neptune above the roar of the waves.

Stance and posture. Movements in presentation. What they tell about you

How you stand when speaking tells a lot about you. It can make or mar your presentation.

The playright, Bernard Shaw (who hid his own shyness behind beautiful diction, Irish wit, splendid bearing, and a full gingery beard), once offered the famous English author H. G. Wells pungent advice after a speech. 'You insisted on having a table; leaning over it on your knuckles; and addressing the contents of your contracted chest to the tablecloth.' Wells had little presence, a piping voice, and had worked in a draper's. Shaw, with perverse Shavian logic, tried to make him stand better by hitting him below the belt. 'Where did you get that attitude? In the shop. . . . When your knuckles touched the cloth, you said unconsciously by reflex action "Anything else today, madam?" Fortunately, you were inaudible. . . .'

Attitudes of mind and body correspond. Your position and pose, how your body and limbs are disposed, consciously or unconsciously convey much to your audience. Since kinesics (body language) has become such a popular study, clients notice this more. The late Ted Ray, a brilliant comedian, though limping bravely after a motor accident, grinned to a friend: 'Never let the public see you down.'

147

A faulty stance often signals what speakers are trying to hide. H. G. Wells's 'horse at the piano' stance was similar to the widespread flippers of the 'seal on the ice-floe'. Both put us off by appearing unctuous, obsequious, and cringing.

Don't lean. It gives you the tortoise-like, head-out-of-shell appearance made a trademark by a famous British TV personality.

The speaker wrestling with his chairback, like a lion-tamer, or using a rostrum like a machine-gun emplacement, is intent on keeping 'em off. You can't win while taking cover.

Hands in the footballer's free-kick position (genital clutch), or arms folded in scowling 'they shall not pass' stance, reinforce fear by acting it out physically.

Speaking, presenting, persuasion, and wooing are related activities—and no man ever wooed with arms folded.

Foot-on-a-chair, hand in a trouser-pocket, haunches hooked sideways on a table all say 'Look how relaxed and casual I am'. OK sometimes, but they can be too offhand if the audience is not prepared to be casual.

Inclined head, finger at mouth, twisting in-turned toe, or standing wide-legged (as if waiting for a wet napkin to be changed)—all these try to win sympathy by infantile winsomeness. They move only the motherly.

Then there are gestures of propitiation, like the body-swaying hands-on-hips position, sometimes performed (generally in advertising agencies) with jacket skirts raised. Anthropologist-zoologist Desmond Morris clearly said that, among the primates, showing the buttocks is an act of submission, with sexual connotations.

Shy speakers under stress sometimes revert to habits previously appropriate. One who clamped his chin on his left shoulder had been, I discovered, an infant violinist. Another who vehemently addressed the floor had stood on the bathside instructing swimmers immersed in the water.

Without realizing it, terrified speakers draw steadily away from their audience, often towards a door. If they back into something they may bounce themselves against it, like a boxer on the ropes. Movement with purpose is desirable. But the perambulating professor, going backwards and forwards across the stage, is running away—nearly.

A presenter becomes stronger as he approaches his audience. He can consciously relax them by drawing back appropriately. Distance is a significant factor in involvement. A restaurant owner instructed his belly dancers, for instance, how close they might approach diners. 'With a titled dignitary in the room, they dance on the stage,' he said. 'If it's councillors, they may dance within four feet. Bankers two feet, and insurance executives at one foot.'

Some low-key presenters try to do the job sitting down. To me, this is an abdication from authority. Standing up signals clearly who 'holds the floor'. Sitting invites interruption and loose discussion.

On the other hand, two of the most hard-hitting speakers I ever encountered in business used the same stance. They were Brian McCabe, at Foote Cone and Belding, and Norman Collins, at ATV. They planted their feet firmly apart, they gripped a wrist decisively with the other hand behind their backs, stuck their heads forwards like fighting cocks, and spoke with the attack of someone bouncing a punchball with his chin.

Nobody ever argued with them. You, too, can stand straight, head up, smile ready, and use your voice at good volume. Try it; it works.

Stink? We don't—much. The suicidal approach to presentation

A young executive of a London PR agency was invited to speak to his local Chamber of Commerce about public relations. I offered him a rehearsal. With the right brief, he could have been impressive. But he did not want any help, thank you.

He cited various hoary criticisms of PR, then set out to prove them fallacious. A negative no-hope-of-winning approach 'They tore me to ribbons,' he admitted ruefully.

Lots of bosses don't much notice the 99 per cent of their operation that goes through smoothly. But they are bedevilled daily by the 1 per cent of people with troubles. Under stress, it is easy for them to be over-impressed by these malcontents.

Such a boss easily becomes increasingly negative and defensive. It is then that he begins to make apologetic public utterances of the kind which I brutally classify as the 'We don't stink—much' argument. It is always a wrong approach.

The French have a proverb for it: *'Qui s'excuse, s'accuse.'* Who excuses himself, accuses himself. As Shakespeare has it: 'And oftentimes excusing of a fault doth make the fault the worse by the excuse.'

A big-time tobacco executive was rehearsing answering questions about a cigarette launch in front of CCTV. His response to the usual anti-smoking questions was good. So I bowled him a fast one: 'Can you please give me five good reasons why cigarette smoking is, in some way or other, beneficial?' He was so used to fending off attack that the friendly enquiry stumped him. For years, he had taken smoking's good points for granted, and never verbalized them. He broke off the CCTV session, sitting down to write himself a list of plus points.

Any presenter who detects himself preparing a 'We don't stink —much' speech should do just this: emphasize the positive, eliminate the negative.

Swearing in presentations. Why it is a damn bad habit

Should you swear, or allow it, in presentations? Does a cuss or two add emphasis to speaking? Or will a naughty word alienate the client and lose business?

The musical film *My Fair Lady* appeared first as the play *Pygmalion*. It became notorious because the heroine Eliza Doolittle had to swear on stage. When a young man invited her to walk across the park, she answered: 'Not bloody likely!'

Very daring, in those days. But since then, speakers, presenters, journalists, playwrights, and TV personalities have pushed the frontiers of profanity right to the edge.

In the *Journal of Communication* recently, three experts revealed that in a sample of everyday American speech, every fourteenth word contained profanity. They divided it into three categories: religious, excretory, and sexual.

Swearing was once a way of putting a curse on something or somebody. We don't take this so seriously today. But people in business still swear for a least five reasons.

1. To add colour and emphasis to a weak vocabulary.

2. To shock, kill boredom, frighten, or motivate.

3. To signal rebellion and freedom from restraint or respect.

4. To vent anger or frustration, sometimes instead of physical violence.

5. Habitually, as psychologists might say, to comply with the mores of their peers (keep up with the boys).

Salty words now appear in everything from business dictation to the *Oxford Dictionary*. Even the four-letter 'F' is hardly frowned upon since author-critic Kenneth Tynan first said it on British TV.

Swearing nevertheless still shocks even broadminded people. The public of the USA was scandalized that President Richard Nixon, outwardly pious, was shown by his tapes to be so profane in private.

Sexual or excretory terms are generally false intensives that can better be omitted. You can offend religious-minded people by taking the Deity's name in vain (but nobody minds if you say 'By heavens!')

My view is that if the client chooses to be profane or obscene, that is his affair. Let him enjoy this verbal rubbish tip as his prerogative. Don't trespass into it in your presentation. It won't pay.

The three American experts summed up: 'It was found that using profanity in a communication has a detrimental effect on

151

the perceived credibility of the communicator.' This applies even more, they said, to females.

Moral: don't bloody swear if you want the b------s to believe you, especially if you're an expletive dame!

T

Tape-recorder techniques for presentation polishing

No presenter should be without his own personal portable tape-recorder, with a spare cassette or two, for rehearsing presentations.

What a self-revelation! In the early days of cheaper recorders, a filling-station man on the Southend Road from London said to me: 'Yus, I know. I bought one of 'em fings. I sund like a flippin' Cockney, doan I? A proper bleedin' barrer boy—and I never noo!' Then the phone rang and, picking it up, he answered in classy London English, self-taught by tape-recorder.

A clergyman wanted to monitor his presentation of the church service, especially the sermon. He recorded it on Sunday morning. Sitting in an armchair after lunch to listen to it critically, he woke to hear himself announcing the final hymn.

The practical way to use a recorder for monitoring your presentation is first to set up the microphone on a table or desk five or six feet away. Stand up and deliver a paragraph or two as if to the presentation audience.

Stop and check whether this is adequately recorded by playing it back. Adjust the recording volume control if necessary. Then record the whole piece, still standing, timing it preferably by stop-watch.

153

Now you can sit back and listen critically. Stop where necessary to amend your script, cut out tongue-twisters, clarify figures, remove unwanted repetition, simplify, add emphasis, and so on.

Repeat this complete process two or three times, and you create a streamlined presentation that you know by aural memory as well from the prompting of your notes or script.

If you want to refresh at other times, possibly you can play the cassette in your car.

If you do not like writing a presentation script, you can work one up on tape by trial and improvement, then have it typed from the latest version. You will then have a script to fit both the facts and your fashion of speaking.

Teams of presenters. Coordinating people for high morale

Uffa Fox, when he was the Cowes sailing companion of Prince Philip, told me 'You must get drunk with a man three nights running, if you want to win yacht races together'.

Similar comradeship (arising from mutual suffering bravely borne) is necessary to make a good presentation team. Work can replace drinking, though many don't rule out the latter.

Two, three, four, or more people thrown together don't necessarily make a team. They can easily create chaos or a minor riot. To achieve teamsmanship, they need:
1. A coordinating trainer or producer.
2. A friendly relationship. One client recently said to two quarrelling presenters: 'I shall wait until one of you kills the other, and then deal myself with the survivor.' How could they hope to win?
3. The best 'batting order'. Think of the client, and what final effect has to be left. It is not a question of who wants to be first or last, but which arrangement will give the best effect.

4. Controlled off-rostrum behaviour. While the presentation continues and the clients are there, everyone is *on stage*. Nervousness, relief, edginess, cynicism, criticism of colleagues, and boredom must all be hidden. The team must all look interested and alert all the time.

5. Good morale. This is created by the leader. The team needs worthwhile tasks, a degree of hard struggle, some success, and not only high standards but sincere appreciation and praise.

Applying these five points will weld a good 'warrior band' of presenters. After that, the rest is inspiration plus perspiration. This was how my teams, year-after-year, won national speaking competitions.

TV's effect on manner in presentation—watch it!

The great British Prime Minister of the last century, William Gladstone, annoyed Queen Victoria because 'He speaks to me as if I was a public meeting'. If he were to reappear today, his exaggerated, long-winded style of presentation would make people laugh.

Styles of speaking and presentation change like dress fashions. Would Churchill's great wartime oratory impress today as it did then? Those who heard the Welsh wizard Lloyd George in latter days thought him high-flown and old-fashioned. Once, he was a spell-binder.

The new manner is more conventional. Thanks to microphones, big voices are not so necessary. Hammy theatrical styles are out. But that is no guarantee that there will not be a swing back in the opposite direction.

Country and western play it cool. Rock-n-rollers scream and shout. Politicians begin to talk rather than orate. What TV pours into every home cannot fail to effect manners in presentation. The man or woman on TV is unconsciously adopted by all of us as setting standards in presentation. The wise presenter keeps an eye on what they are doing.

How are popular science programmes put over? What techniques are used in presenting works of art? Is there something to learn from business items? Have scoreboards anything extra to tell us about business presentations?

Look at programmes with a cold, objective eye. Occasionally include those you normally miss, perhaps with the sound off. TV sets a great pace, and business presentation must keep up.

Time limits. How to stay happily inside them and please all

A leading European management consultant was lecturing to several hundred businessmen at the Royal Lancaster Hotel, in London. The eloquence poured from him. The minutes ticked on. I wondered if he knew the time.

Then, unseen by the audience, an assistant appeared at the back of the hall. He lifted high a large board numbered 5. It meant minutes. Shortly it was changed to 2, then 0. The lecturer stopped and relieved waiters began serving lunch.

Staying within time limits causes some presenters extraordinary difficulty. Even at a 'Time Management' seminar not long ago, delegates grumbled that the eminent author-expert overran four times a day for two days.

Good time-keeping is essential. Even if a presentation is intended to be immortal, there's no need for it to go on for ever.

Research shows that the only human muscle that never tires is the tongue, and an American politician's wife proved it thus:

I love its gentle warble,
I love its fluent flow.
I love to wind my tongue up
And let the darn thing go.

According to Sir Edwin Leather at an Institute of Marketing dinner, a verger told a visiting bishop who asked how long to preach: 'We have no record in this parish of any sinner repenting after the first 10 minutes.'

The Etonian jazz trumpeter, Humphrey Littleton, recorded of his school: 'In company with 95 per cent of my fellows, I was prone to a physical condition which came on in chapel with remorseless punctuality when the sermon lasted longer than eight minutes. . . . We used to call it Numb Bum.'

Abraham Lincoln's famous Gettysburg Address ('. . . all men are created equal, etc.'—266 words) lasted just over two minutes.

Rehearse your material out loud against a stopwatch and allow that it will run 10 per cent longer if things go well on the day.

Signals in great variety are offered to keep speakers to time: green starting lights, yellow warning lights, red stopping lights; watches that buzz, clocks that bleep. The Romans used a water-clock that dripped for 20 minutes. Some speakers drip too long. To signal a time limit in competitions, I removed my spectacles at a certain moment as I sat among the audience. My speakers knew this meant seven minutes.

The best time discipline comes from within, when a speaker learns to rely on his own time-piece. He can place it on the table in front of him, or twist it on his wrist to show more readily.

For a long presentation, write the running time at the foot of each page of notes. Adjust to these figures as you progress.

At the Media Circle's annual presentation weekend, when 50 young advertising men and women practice at Caius College, Cambridge, the students generously presented me with a handsome brass hand-bell, engraved with the best possible advice on timing. It said in Latin, *praestate dicete et tacete*—'Stand up, speak up, and shut up'. The final words are imperative.

Training in business speaking and presentation. Why it pays

Most men and women in business were taught four things at school: to read, to write, to figure—and to shut up.

Radio, records, tapes, TV, films, public loud-speaker announcements, police loud-hailers, and the general regimentation of life make it possible to listen a lot without saying anything.

Today a citizen can rise from his bed and reach his place of work, perhaps several miles distant, without himself uttering a single word. Maybe he doesn't need to speak at any time all day. No wonder some youngsters (and more mature folk, too) are so inarticulate!

Speaking to a group lags behind other personal skills. But training can raise it to equal other levels. Here are seven reasons why companies should obtain presentation training for their people:

1. *Presentation training makes managers and salesmen worth more.* People are expensive and good ones are hard to find. It pays better to increase their effectiveness and hang onto them, rather than to hire others.

A London advertisement representative of a provincial newspaper trained in his spare time with my speaking group. One lunch time he made a speech in a Fleet Street club. Shortly afterwards, on the strength of that one utterance, he was offered the advertisement managership at a national weekly journal—a considerable promotion.

2. *Training helps executives to become articulate.* The higher a person climbs in business, the greater the need to inform and persuade other people. One constant criticism of bosses is: 'He never tells you. He seems to think you ought to know.' Communication by defection.

The man who improves his communication skills is often promoted shortly after. Three months after attending a presentation course in Brussels, the European treasurer of an international

159

organization telephoned me. He had been given world responsibility.

3. *Training helps groups to work together better.* People working together today often have joint responsibility as a decision making unit. Speaking training promotes comradeship and improves cooperation. It instils better group disciplines, which aid logical thinking and speed working.

An international company in confectionery recently put its research and development scientists on an in-house presentation course simply to improve their communication inside the group.

4. *Speaking training uncovers hidden talents.* A woman secretary in an international training organization was drafted onto one of their all-comers presentation courses to make up suddenly depleted numbers. Normally an efficient but far from talkative person, she took to presentation like a hawk to flying. Within the year she became assistant to the managing director of the organization, and then a lecturer in her own right.

Selecting personnel for promotion is a gamble where bosses can't afford not to pick winners. Group presentation training is a way of highlighting the best. It uncovers unexpected talents.

5. *Training prepares people for promotion.* Experts in job techniques often cannot put their knowledge across adequately to others. The classic case is the top salesman whom management wants to promote to district or area manager. Can he handle a team of erstwhile colleagues?

An external all-comers presentation and speaking course gives him a chance to develop poise, clarity, and confidence without his colleagues barracking. He becomes more articulate and returns better able to handle new responsibilities.

6. *Speaking training adds value to jobs.* Enrichment of the daily job is a way of showing an employee that he or she is appreciated by the company. Presentation training is an ego-boosting operation that does this.

The social spin-off can be considerable, too. One executive who took training 20 years ago recently became chairman of an exclusive British club which stages prestigious celebrity lunches.

7. *Better business speaking swings millions, sometimes in minutes.* Fat contracts can hang on the effectiveness of only a few minutes

160

speaking. In the face-to-face confrontation, training pays off in profits worth hundreds of times what it costs.

An Irish manager, who first kicked against going on my course, nevertheless set out to get value from it. Now chief executive, he recently spoke so well on radio and TV that his company's shares were pushed up points overnight.

You can pick up a lot about the various strokes in swimming by reading a book. But actually to learn to swim well, you must get into the water. Nobody can swim on dry land; nobody can learn to sway a non-existent audience. You must practice on real people, preferably in the non-risk atmosphere of a good course.

Translation brings problems especially when simultaneous

In Madrid, a tactful Spanish translator confided into his microphone: 'Our English presenter is now beginning a joke. I cannot translate it for you. But please continue to look interested. And please laugh—*now!*'

Other nationals are very polite about it, but with notable exceptions English and American presenters travelling abroad lag behind others in their knowledge of languages.

Somebody therefore has to translate, which bedevils communication. Inspired trade names, for example, notoriously may turn out to be unusably vulgar. A perfume romantically labelled 'mist' in English, in German means 'manure'.

Presentations should always be made, if humanly possible, in a language both the speaker and the audience readily understand. Using a translator consumes a minimum of twice the time and often ten times the patience. In high-level business presentations, simultaneous translation brings even greater hazards.

For a start, English is a short language. French is longer, and

161

German longer still, with verbs in what Englishmen regard as curious places. When presenting in English for simultaneous translation, it is essential to pause between phrases and sentences for the translators to catch up.

A British business author was rattling away enthusiastically to 350 people (representing 22 nationalities) at an institute in Zurich. Inside their glass cubicles, the translators into French and German did their best—but. . . . Picking up my headphones, I listened with one ear to the French. The lady translator had almost given up. It was the fast-talking English presenter's fault. Mademoiselle was just doing alternate sentences.

Politeness often deceives the naive English presenter abroad. When Japanese smile and nod, it does not necessarily mean agreement or even understanding. It simply signals that the audience are courteously aware that you are saying something.

The presenter being translated from English must also avoid slang, idiomatic phrases, and puzzling allusions. His expressions must be simple to translate and he must talk slowly . . . slowly.

Used-up feeling after presentation.
How to dispel the depression

A used-up feeling of personal uselessness and unworthiness can come over even the bounciest of presenters after the job is done—even if you've won the business. Why?

In maternity, doctors recognize post-natal depression in the mother as a not uncommon risk; sometimes it takes extreme forms. After breaking world records, athletes experience similar doldrums. Following exams, even redbrick college students feel blue. It's as well to realize that this is normal, and that if you feel that you did disastrously, it probably was not so bad as all that.

In my taxi to Amsterdam airport, after the excitement and endeavour of running my first three-day presentation course in English for top Dutch executives, I suddenly felt 'the trip' was over. Life abruptly turned flat and grey. Fortunately I knew that symptom of old and what to take for it.

The energy output that wins audiences drains you intellectually and emotionally. Afterwards, as if with a hole in the bottom of your soul, you feel sucked down by a whirlpool to black depths. This is performance's own peculiar hangover. It can happen after a sales conference, a tough interview, or even athletics. Don't accept your own bad verdict at this time. After his third

163

world record in 40 days, Sebastian Coe said 'there was a feeling of colossal emptiness!'

You must reject dejection and find your own first aid: booze, a doze, music, TV, chat, a stroll, a meal, companionship, light reading, maybe even a sleeping pill. Normal sanity will be restored as soon as possible. Some find that exercise is the best therapy. 'The trick is,' says Whit Hobbs, creative consultant to *The New Yorker* and the Sperry Corporation, 'to get yourself as tired physically as you are emotionally and mentally. Don't take a taxi to your hotel. Walk. Better still, run.'

You win some, you miss some. Most important of all is to keep your spirits up to try again another day.

V

Venue of your presentation. Check it in advance

Presenting new point-of-sale posters to the marketing director of a client company, a bright young creative man had a seductive idea. He physically stuck them to the director's clean, newly-decorated office walls. They looked great. But dismantling the show pulled off dinner-plate patches of wall paint, cost a complete redecoration, and almost lost the account.

For presenting, generally there's no place like home. There are no travelling problems for your presenters and your props. You have the advantage of being hosts completely in control of hospitality. If anything threatens to go wrong, you have your whole organization as back-up, with immediate knowledge of where to go for help.

However, home is not always convenient, largely because architects, builders, and furniture designers seem to know little about presentation. Windows are placed where audiences can gaze at a passing scene; doors so that people enter behind the speaker's back; lights are hung on immensely long leads so that you crouch to see across the table; or to give height to a low room, the table is made to suit dwarfs. Armless chairs can be hell to sit on after half an hour. Some have joke backlegs, which

165

totally collapse if you tilt them. At one top London advertising agency, the new plastic upholstery emitted such relentless raspberries that the whole embarrassing suite had to be replaced.

Posh presentation rooms are sometimes so infested with gimmickry that you need a pilot's licence to fly them. Sometimes the place is so acoustically dead (for films and audio-visual purposes) that a speaker six feet away needs a microphone to be properly heard.

One West End of London presentation room sends so much ventilation up your trouser legs that your spectacles wobble in the wind.

After presentations on home ground (which sometimes reveal more about the company than intended) there are hotels and conference centres. The first question then is not when do you want the room, but when is it available. Three months, six months, or even a year ahead may not be too soon to enquire. Can the audience reach it conveniently? Are there bedrooms for those from long distances? It is too homely or too luxurious? What will it cost? These are secondary questions.

See it before you hire it. Try to visit it again a week or so in advance to assess possibilities. Arrive overnight or at least an hour or two before starting time on the day.

In some hotels it is necessary to raise hell fast to get things right. They loudly proclaim their conference facilities but really are interested only in selling drinks, meals, and beds. Their porters' ideas of what will suit you are bizarre.

Have a clear idea of what you want and insist on being given it. The success of your show depends on you being effective as your own stage manager. It is your show that is at risk. Do not take rudeness or reluctance. Call the manager soon rather than late.

Conference centres are better. They know more about your needs. But sometimes they are vast, remote, unpeopled, and difficult to find your way about. You may need to put up brightly coloured signposts, posters, and directions.

When you are presenting on the client's premises, tread even more softly. Try to see the room in advance, but unless you are lucky you will be unlikely to rehearse there. Telephone the day before to remind them of the date. I was kept waiting in the snow

166

for an hour outside locked premises of a national company in Coventry. 'Is it today?' queried the manager. 'OK. Shove the office furniture back to make some space, and start when you like.'

A gracious and well-arranged venue can improve your presentation tremendously. But whatever the conditions, never criticize them to the owners. A canteen, a garage, or a claustrophobic cellar—goodwill, ingenuity, and a pasted-on smile can make them work. You just have to be that much more brilliant yourself.

Visual aids are an extra responsibility. Ten commandments

About 80 per cent of what we perceive comes through the eyes. When we show as well as tell, people recall three times as much. A Chinese sage is supposed to have said that a picture is worth a thousand words. Certainly it is true that nowadays a presentation without visuals is as suspect as a business lunch without drinks.

Visuals add punch. Their variety and colour maintain interest. They aid compression. They illustrate what words can hardly say and they cater for those in your audience whose perception is more visual than auditory. But managing visuals is an extra responsibility for you as the presenter. Some people find in them an inbuilt awkwardness and antagonism that is said to exist at times in many inanimate objects.

Accepting that mainly for the benefit of the audience, but also partly for yourself, you must have visuals, how can you handle them most effectively? Here are ten commandments common to most of them.

1. *Don't have too many visuals.* They confuse the audience and distract from your message. 'Is this visual really necessary?' is therefore a good question. Culling can make the message more vivid.

At the other extreme, a single pathetic visual in a longish presentation gives an impoverished impression, though there may be occasions when one magnificent visual will carry the whole show.
2. *Keep the visuals in keeping.* Grimly functional black lettering won't fit with a fashion show where the chairs are golden and the curtains silk. Comic sketches won't do for the solemn business of applying for some serious planning permission. Have visuals fitting for their purpose.
3. *Use colour for variety.* The more prosaic the general appearance of a visual, the more need for a stripe of colour, a bright star, or ringed item to entertain the eye.

TV is in colour. Snapshots are in colour. Magazines and newspapers are in colour. Visual aids must use colour too. Colour is a desirable element of communication.
4. *Make them large, put them high.* The Highway Code in Britain expects drivers to be able to read a three-inch high car registration number at 25 yards. Bad visuals often ask the audience to read quarter-inch letters at 25 feet, and they can't. It should be one inch high at least.

Lettering gets too small when you try to pack too much onto a transparency, a slide, or a flipchart sheet. Scribble a sample, with a thick pen, stick it on the wall, and pace off the maximum audience distance. Can you see it clearly?

Also, is it high enough above the heads of other members of the audience for all to see it?
5. *Get the light right.* A cardboard chart backed against a bright window just makes a silhouette. An overhead projector shining onto a sunlit screen shows a ghostly picture.

Light must shine on the right place. A shiny surface on a chart can reflect a blinding beam through an audience. Check the light and get it right.
6. *Watch the sight lines.* An artist sketching instant caricatures in a cabaret had to rip them off the easel to show around to the audience, many of whom were behind her. She was aware of their sight lines. In contrast, many presenters unconcernedly stand in the way of their visuals, while polite audiences fail to protest. Ask *yourself* (not the audience) about every visual 'Can they see it comfortably?'

168

7. *Retain the initiative over the aid.* The creative director of a New York advertising agency made a presentation with numerous blow-ups of bits of masterpiece paintings as visuals. He ranged them round the wall as he introduced them. Long before he finished, none of us was listening. We were gazing spellbound at the pictures.

Never show a visual until you need it. Never leave it in sight after you have finished with it. Cover it up, switch it off, or walk in front of it. Otherwise, it will probably steal your limelight.

8. *Don't talk to the visual.* An electronics engineer flashed up a complicated circuit diagram, and talked directly to it, his back to the audience, for 20 minutes. He was fascinated.

The visual is intended primarily to aid the audience, not the presenter. It is bad manners to turn your back. Pull your eyes off your visual and talk to the audience about it.

9. *Go for the greatest impact.* Visuals become stronger as they move on from figures to graphs, to diagrams, to pictures, to objects, and to actions. If you want a visual to hit hard, take it along this path as far as the basic idea can be persuaded to go.

Verbal visuals, especially abstract words, are generally the most flaccid of all. When one shows a word describing something we cannot see, touch, hear, taste, or smell, it is virtually value-less. Integrity, ambition, industriousness, planning, and so on are cloud-words, which lull everyone into a dreamland of totally forgettable vagueness. In certain circumstances, word visuals can usefully consist of checklists of actions-to-be-taken.

10. *Rehearse, rehearse.* Whatever form your visual takes, it will have in common with all others the propensity for tripping you up. Even turning a flipchart sheet can be done neatly and with good timing, badly so that it cockles or rips, or disastrously so that the whole lot cascades to the ground.

Too often a presenter approaches a projector and asks 'How do you switch this thing on?' He should find out in advance. Otherwise he labels himself an amateur.

Try out your visuals where they are to be used. Check that they function well in this venue. Rehearse till you have everything slick and unobtrusively right.

As well as a presenter of the spoken word, you are now a

conjuror, a juggler, and a showman. See that the visuals work for you, not you for them.

Voice. Qualities to use to make yours more interesting and persuasive

'I have heard the sheerest nonsense talked, and watched it being believed, simply because it was delivered with the voice of a text book:' said presentation man, Ralph L. Finn. 'And I have heard sound common sense being ignored, simply because it was uttered diffidently.'

Vocal style is most easily exemplified in print by citing public figures. A woman with a high voice, for example, can sound like a schoolgirl. When the Queen learnt to pitch her speechmaking voice lower, she became a much better speaker. Of male Premiers, Ramsay Macdonald was a charismatic Scot with a voice as beautiful as a church organ. Most presenters can't compare with such models as these. But they should be aware of how the voice can be used, and the general effects of change.

Clarity of enunciation (good use of the lips, tongue, and teeth) is a characteristic of many Scots that makes them *sound* definite and clear-minded. The Welsh have music in their voices. The Irish have a gift of phrase and soft charm that suggests wit.

Many young presenters do not use enough voice. It is as if they feel that to make a mistake inaudibly is better than to do so clearly. Good volume gives the speaker confidence, and stirs the audience's brain cells. Speak up with apparent confidence and only whisper (for dramatic effect) so-called secrets or information you are suggesting is confidential.

Don't drop the volume in a fade-away at sentence ends. Don't keep the chin too close to the chest. Don't make your sounds half-way down the throat like a hoarse Cockney costermonger,

170

but produce the tone up in the head so that it rings out like the bell-tones of a declaiming actor.

Pace has its uses. Speaking rapidly with clarity gives the message urgency. Gabbling and mumbling, however, makes listeners feel you are ashamed of what you are saying and want to finish as quickly as possible. Speaking slowly and easily is a good way to begin a presentation, to give listeners a chance to tune in. Speaking slowly with emphasis makes a fact or figure sound important—a useful technique for any vital part of your presentation. And timing, the clever use of pauses, adds tremendously to impact.

The final main factor in getting variety and interest into the voice is pitch—whether you speak on almost one note (a monotonous habit of many shy businessmen) or whether you use variations between high and low. The hectoring, bullying speeches of Nazi officials were delivered in high hysterical voices. High pitch in any language provokes excitement, as every broadcasting sports commentator frequently demonstrates. At the other extreme, pull your voice down as low as it will reasonably go and you impress with the solemnity of your utterance—not a bad thing when speaking of the serious aspects of a client's business.

Perhaps 'the voice of a textbook', as mentioned above by Ralph Finn, is misleading. No presenter should talk like a brochure. But your voice should sound confident, controlled, and well-modulated according to what you are saying. The delivery of your presentation will then match the sound common sense of the content.

Welcoming the visiting client and setting the right mood

Near the famous Ritz Hotel, in Piccadilly, London, I took the lift from a lively young advertising agency's reception area to meet their top bosses. As the doors slid open, I was confronted with three smiling men in a neat row, bowing slightly, each with right hand purposefully extended to shake.

Dilemma! It was obviously a test. I gripped them firmly— middle, left, right—in order of company rank, chief executive first. 'He knows the precedence!' they laughed. A fun welcome.

Those who bustle unhindered daily into their buildings should give thought to how the visiting client is treated. Entering the building 20 minutes in advance for a Birmingham appointment, a rich new client was so unhappily held up by the company's gnomish liftman and dragon receptionist that he arrived late. He was touchy till after lunch.

Irritable commissionaires, bored and yawning receptionists swapping last night's gossip, and tough security men in glass-sided gatehouses create the worst atmosphere. They are frequently so obsequious to their bosses that nobody in the company realizes the bad image they project to strangers.

Good reception people are worth their weight in swing doors.

173

At Seltrust Engineering in Clerkenwell, London, a self-trained reception executive (she deserves such a description) uncannily knows everyone by name and jumps up to shake hands with them. At Daf Trucks in Marlow, a welcome-board at the office entrance displays your name in white letters. Any client at either place feels warmly wanted and expected.

If you are printing banknotes, sorting diamonds, or showing the crown jewels, tight security is morally good. It prevents wrong-doing. But other companies must decide whether the entrance is a portcullis to be guarded against foes or a fairway for friends.

Worst hazards for visiting clients are lack of car-parking in a strange place, the harassed girl at the switchboard who glances back anxiously over one shoulder at you, and deserted front offices.

Welcome is the digits of two extended hands. I mean that your visitor wants five things before meeting you and five after.

1. Premises easy to find. Are they well labelled? Do you send new callers a clear map?

2. Parking that is neither a panicky voyage of discovery nor a squeeze-in driving test.

3. Pleasant greeting at reception, by name if possible, and no demeaning signing of a 'Prison Visitors' book.

4. Peg for coat and possibly hat, where they are easily recoverable on leaving.

5. Prompt call to, and meeting with you, the visitor's contact.

On the other welcoming hand, after being greeted, the visitor has five more possible wants once you've met:

1. Toilet. Apart from calls of nature, hands get grubby on newspaper ink and public transport, face needs freshening, and hair-combing and tie-straightening are required.

2. Telephone. A quick call about something urgent can remove worry from your visitor's mind and make him better able to concentrate on your business.

3. Refreshment, generally coffee.

4. Comfortable seating. Low armchairs are tiresome to rise from. A normal-height chair, with arms, is a kindness and a courtesy.

5. Finally, a punctual start to business with everyone present is the prime politeness.

174

The welcoming process merges into general hospitality. The client should not be over-fussed, nor abandoned or mislaid. He should be made to feel at home—but still as an honoured guest, not one of the family expected to fend for himself.

The emotional tone established can tip the balance in the final business judgement, either against or for.

Will to win. Five ways to get muscles on yours

You were handed a promise in the title of this book: *How to Make Effective Business Presentations—and Win!* The last word is vital. Winning in presentations means achieving the effect you desire. You should never rely on it happening by accident. There are five rules of winning.

1. You can't hit the target if you don't know what you're aiming at. Discover and define your objective clearly and early.

2. Boxers who keep fit but don't fight championships find it hard to win after a year or more out of the ring. Continually practice your presentation-winning techniques in real-life situations.

3. 'Same again' won't do. Every occasion is different. Prepare with meticulous precision, realizing each presentation is a new one.

4. Make winning habitual. Train yourself in it. Deserve it. Establish success as a customary experience. The prospect of winning should never scare you. Don't be frightened of your own aggression. Be ready to *enjoy* the success you achieve.

5. A horse runs till it tires: a thoroughbred goes till it drops. Develop muscles on your will to win. Work on your emotional stamina. *Never give up.*

Mike Brearley (who brilliantly captained the England Cricket XI to beat the Australians and retain the Ashes with two 'impossible' Test Match wins) advises us to be resilient to minor setbacks. 'In difficulties I have, like a toddler learning to walk, picked myself up and carried on without self-criticism, and scored runs.'

Forty psychologists accompanied various East European teams of winners at the Moscow Olympics. Such trainers know how to make a weight-lifter, for example, pick up a heavier load than he believes possible.

In the professions, winners teach themselves how to bring the will to its optimum for the time of performance. Introverts are often too tense and need relaxing; easy-minded extroverts have to be 'psyched up' for the fight.

Winning in business presentations is a technique to study. It is a tough one. Make it your habit.

Women presenters. When they can do better than men

When the Advertising Association's country-wide public speaking competition was won five years running by the Regent Advertising Club of London, our different annual teams of three presenters always included one young woman. This gave us considerable advantage over competing teams made up of just three men. We often found that our lady competitor was more commonsense and practical, and not so likely to bore us with lofty abstract generalizations as the men.

A good woman speaker is always valuable in a presentation team. A pretty smile, nice figure, suitable neat clothes, well-groomed hair—these are advantages that men normally cannot match.

A lady speaker may have disadvantages, too. Having a small voice sometimes makes a woman better at talking than speaking,

176

at conversation rather than oratory. Often you don't hear a girl speaker properly until you give her a microphone.

Some equable ladies do not, it seems, rouse their own emotions so readily as some men. This can render them too quiet, too tame, and not animated enough. At such times they leave audiences cool.

We accidentally discovered the cure when somebody was provocatively outspoken to a young woman named Liz just before she spoke in a competition. She mounted the platform with pink cheeks, hammered the audience, and won the Best Speaker's cup.

Women can make notable speeches when there is need. Four centuries ago, Queen Elizabeth of England had been warned that it was dangerous for her to visit troops at Tilbury, on the River Thames, waiting for the Spanish Armada and invasion. But she went, as she said, 'being resolved, in the midst and heat of the battle, to live or die amongst you all. . . .'

'I know I have but the body of a weak and feeble woman,' she went on. 'But I have the heart and stomach of a King, and of a King of England, too; and think foul scorn that any prince of Europe should dare to invade the borders of my realms.'

She forecast a famous victory—and won it. Use a woman presenter whenever possible. She will add an extra dimension to your communication.

Writing for persuasive speaking. Avoiding unspeakable presentation scripts

When I first sat down at my little Remington portable to type a BBC talk, it came out virtually unspeakable. The language was compressed news-style, not spoken English.

Similarly, persuasive presentation English does not spring from the style used for business memos or concise letters and reports. Wrestling at rehearsing 'literary' scripts will never make them into the kind of language you use when talking to people.

Alistair Cooke, the famous 'Letter from America' broadcaster, found the way round this difficulty by talking aloud to himself—and taking it down on his typewriter. His sentences are eminently speakable—which is what you want, too, for a presentation.

What's the difference between written and spoken language? In spoken English, you can safely be a little less than pedantically grammatical. Aim at being clear, concise, and acceptably correct. (Remember that you have vocal inflections to aid your meaning, which are not possible in writing.)

You can make sentences shorter by omitting verbs. 'Not much money, but a lot of fun,' a presenter might say. The single word 'Not' replaces the fuller phrase 'You will not receive much. . . .'

You can be colloquial at times, or even use slang. If it be brought in at the right moment, audiences will savour the salty brevity.

You can drop the remote ritual of using the third person: 'the client', 'the company', 'One'. You can talk in straightforward style about 'you' and 'we' or 'us'.

You can also use repetitive constructions for a stronger dramatic emphasis: 'We shall not do so and so. Neither shall we do thus and thus. What we *shall* do is. . . .'

If in doubt, a good test for expressing anything in spoken English is to ask yourself 'How would I say it to a friend?' Certainly you would not use stiff literary language.

However you compose your presentation, always read or rehearse it out loud to remove verbal man-traps: for instance, words that have the same sound but different meanings, or can be misunderstood as improper.

Tongue twisters often look OK on paper. 'Sophisticated certification systems. . . .' Cut it down into something simpler, in case you stumble saying it.

False chattiness does not transmute the written into the spoken word. 'OK?' 'Right' 'You see' 'You know' generally sound like irritating mannerisms.

Some people play the piano, as we say, by ear. They are often free, spontaneous, and very pleasing players. For presentation scripts that sound spontaneous, we need to *write* by ear.

Xenophobia is one for presenters to stand on its head

At a presentation in English to a multi-national audience in Amsterdam, a vintage British director of a nationalized industry said that his customers included this company and that, 'and old Uncle Tom Cobley and all.' Several Europeans present looked puzzled.

The phrase was a symptom of his basic xenophobia (dislike of foreigners). The UK, to him, was an island of wisdom surrounded by oceans of foreign fools who didn't understand everyday English.

Over a drink that evening a charming Dutchman asked what the phrase meant. I explained the English folk song 'Widdecombe Fair'. Somebody borrowed Tom Pierce's grey mare to go to the fair 'with Bill Brewer, Jan Stewer, Peter Gurney, Peter Davey, Dan'l Widdon, 'Arry 'Awk, and old Uncle Tom Cobley and all'—eight riders for one horse! It was a joke, but in brief it meant 'everybody'. The Dutchman nodded. Next day he started using the expression.

The more you learn about other nationalities, the richer your understanding of human nature. As a presenter, you have to learn to like the ways of audiences outside the UK. In Finland and

181

Sweden they are stony-faced, but no less attentive. In Russia, you may be drawing your presentation to a close when you discover that a large portion of the audience is totally new. You have to imitate the old-time cinema and give a continuous performance by starting again directly you finish.

The good intentions of the manager of the Wembley Conference Centre misfired at a Frankfurt presentation. As it was June, he suggested letting the Germans sit comfortably with jackets off. 'Ach, nein!' That would not show proper respect.

'So we sat very formally, as though in a board room . . . and after 20 minutes the meeting got going and they talked freely.'

At the other extreme, Sir Harold Gillies, wearing his robes of a Fellow of the Royal College of Surgeons of England in Rio de Janeiro, was upset by lively chatter in his overflowing audience. Not till later did he learn that in Brazil this is a compliment. Silence to Brazilians shows lack of interest.

Never expect to achieve overnight success in presenting to different cultures, even inside the UK. Study your audiences. Ask help and advice. Be courteous and grateful. Strangers can become friends and customers, too.

You are often your own best visual aid

A well-cut suit can be worth a thousand words when presenting for new business, says an advertising journal. Lord Chesterfield in his day said similarly: 'A man's fortune (his luck) is frequently decided by his first address (manner and appearance). If pleasing, others at once conclude he has merit. But if ungraceful, they decide against him.'

In a presentation, you are often your own best visual aid. And this may go beyond your neat suit, brisk manner, and pleasant voice. The right reassuring smile can be worth a fortune.

Your appearance can also include anything personal which you carry, use or wear. For instance, hats. Speaking on industrial safety at a conference, a delegate wore a miner's safety helmet on stage with good effect.

A yachtsman's cap, a habitual buttonhole flower, a breast-pocket handkerchief, and a white jacket are all acceptable in suitable circumstances.

Strongly framed spectacles give weight to your face. Contact lenses help a woman look younger and possibly more attractive, though glasses can be considered more businesslike.

183

Even a major physical handicap can be stage-managed to save embarrassment. American President Franklin D. Roosevelt, crippled by polio, always arranged to be already seated when the journalists came in for his press conference.

Think of yourself in the role of a visual aid to your presentation, somebody with the task of helping the audience with appearance as well as words. Spare them embarrassment, make them comfortable, and inspire their confidence.

Youthfulness (used with care) helps a presenter's acceptability

'I look so young that people think I'm a kid,' complained a young Manchester executive to me. 'They'd reckon I was brilliant if I appeared 20 years older.'

It is easy to blame one's age. 'Youth is a blunder,' quipped Benjamin Disraeli. 'Manhood a struggle; Old Age a regret.'

A wise head on young shoulders can make up for its youthfulness by showing deference and good manners to the older and more experienced. Even if they do appear to be stick-in-the-mud fuddy-duddies, nothing is gained by telling them so, and less by letting the thought show in your facial expression.

When the presenter is noticeably younger than the client, and his authority might be impugned by it, raise the *average* age of the team by including an older person. A grey-haired chairman can be an asset.

The younger presenter is probably more optimistic about new ideas, but more limited in experience than his seniors. He must appreciate that they, in turn, are likely to be cautious because they know more than he does about what *can't* be done.

The presenter who is obviously senior to his audience enjoys increased authority and persuasiveness—provided he does not demonstrate that he is out-of-touch.

To be between extremes is the best bet. Such a person has more information than the young, more stamina than the old, and more steady momentum than either. The young presenter can comfort himself that these qualities are rapidly coming his way.

'You.' Using the most hypnotic word in presentation

As every clever writer of mail-selling letters knows, the word 'you' is one of the most compelling and hypnotic that can be addressed to any audience, whether in writing or speaking.

That witty columnist Alan Brien wrote about 'you' magic in the *New Statesman* in words which he gave me permission to quote. 'Among my friends', he said, 'there seems to be an exceptionally high proportion of compulsive talkers and infrequent listeners.' (Definition of a presentation audience!)

He went on to describe the ploy he uses to make them listen. 'I simply break into the flow with some such remark as "I met someone the other day who very much reminded me of you" or "who you would have been fascinated to talk to."'

The unfailing 'you' approach! Talking from the point of view of the audience's self-interest.

At the end of his story, Alan Brien said, the friends sit looking puzzled and ask: 'But what has that got to do with *me?*'

Alan Brien then exorcises the spell by replying: 'Absolutely nothing, you egotistical monster, but I knew the only way of capturing your attention was to give you a starring role in the opening sentence.'

The same technique can be employed without the rough rebuff. Use the word 'you' sincerely and you have a master-key for opening up the minds, hearts, and pockets of your presentation audiences.

Your own name. Making it well known through presentation

You would not be human if you did not wish your name to be better known, and well thought of, in your particular area of commerce or industry. A few wish to remain obscure and have no difficulty. Others seem to be torn by contrary desires to be unknown but famous—like Lawrence of Arabia or Sir James (*Peter Pan*) Barrie. They need to master the strange knack of backing accidentally into the limelight.

What about ordinary self-publicity for good business reasons or a good cause? Good self-presentation is probably something that you owe your business or associates.

Do you wish to see your name heading the title of a partnership or company? Featured as the keynote speaker at a conference? Published in industry journals as the contributor of important articles? Appearing perhaps on a book as author or headlined in newspapers?

In every trade, industry, and technology there are people who make a name. Some start late in life, like Grandma Moses, who became famous in the USA as a popular painter at an age when others retire. Some start young. A millionaire property developer told me how he began as a boy carting a heavy amplifier on a butcher's delivery bicycle, with a basket and a small front wheel. 'I got tired of shoving the bike,' he said, 'so I bought a car, but was too young to drive it. I hired an older boy to take me around—and I've had a chauffeur ever since.'

There are many peaks of fame and as many routes to the top as paths up the mountains. But four points help tremendously.

1. Be strong and strive hard at doing a good job. Men at the top have phenomenal stamina and capacity for work. Based on anything but good work, fame crumbles shamefully, as newspapers often record.

2. Be prepared to take advantage of legitimate publicity opportunities. As has been said:

He who whispers down a well
About the goods he has to sell,
Will never make as many dollars
As he who climbs a tree and hollers.

Lowell Thomas, the world-travelling American lecturer, maintained that the ability to make an effective presentation was a short cut to distinction. Today this includes effective apppearance on radio and TV. It pays, too, to get your portrait into print. People remember faces better than names.

3.   Stick to one developing line. 'Jack of all trades and master of none' has been a criticism for centuries. Like any other product, a personality is best advertised through one unique selling proposition.

Author of many books, Hilaire Belloc advised the young writer to concentrate on one subject. At 20, say, write about the earthworm. Continue with worms all your life, said Belloc, and at 60 you will have callers consulting you as the world's worm expert.

4.   Allow yourself newsworthy eccentricities. Nelson is famous for putting his telescope to his blind eye. Professor Einstein for wearing no socks. Henry Moore for his statues with holes. Cartoonists, the media, and ordinary people love to chew over such gossip fodder. Clients, too, like to be connected with a known personality. If yours is a name worth dropping, keep it up!

Z

Zeal and enthusiasm are the final essentials. How to get them

A young man with gingery hair, a jutting jaw, a fierce glance, who paced up and down a platform out of doors, speaking with a lisping impediment, held the crowd at his first parliamentary constituency—'even when they did not understand what he said,' reported a newspaper of those days. His name was Winston S. Churchill. The public was hypnotized by his zeal and enthusiasm—qualities that would make many a pale presentation go better.

'The prospective client is seeking people who radiate confidence, good cheer, and expertise,' wrote Eric Webster. 'This impression will not be conveyed by those who are not only worried about what they have to say, but unskilled in the techniques of how to say it.' An essential ingredient of the technique that Webster wanted are two qualities possessed in excess by the Ancient Greeks—zeal and enthusiasm.

Zeal is a Greek word for fervour, ardour, exuberance, verve, elan. *Enthusiasm* is also from the Greek, meaning possessed by a god. 'Nothing great was ever achieved without enthusiasm,' wrote the American author, Ralph Waldo Emerson. And the English statesman, Lord Balfour, said 'Enthusiasm moves the world'.

A presentation made without enthusiasm is like a lukewarm

189

dinner served on a cold plate. Heat makes a mediocre meal more acceptable, but cold dishes congeal desire.

Stuck with a cold fish in his team, the producer of a presentation can sandwich him between two lively ones to provide contrast; he can pep up his script and visuals so that his hot message contrasts with the cool manner; he can bully and rehearse him into greater excitement—or drop him from the show. Maybe he is better at doing some quiet back-up job.

Enthusiasm must, of course, be tempered to the size and style of the audience. A small group of intellectual executives don't want to be raved at. They will tend to assume that zeal denies knowledge, providing heat in place of illumination.

Zeal need not be noisy, however. Quiet intensity is very persuasive in certain circumstances. But fire in the belly there must be, whether it flares or is banked for slow burning.

Act enthusiastically and you will begin to feel enthusiastic. It is only the heat of enthusiasm that can bring you the response to a presentation which every presenter prays for, meaning you've sold the proposition—and won!